VOLUME 3

Drumset Essentials

PETER ERSKINE

Afro-Caribbean Section by Aaron Serfaty

Copyright © MMIII Alfred Publishing Co., Inc.
All rights reserved. Printed in USA.
ISBN 0-7390-3430-8 (Book)
ISBN 0-7390-3431-6 (Book and CD)

Cover Photograph: Karen Miller

Contents

About the Authors

Peter Erskine has been a student of the drums since the age of four. He is known for his love of working in different musical contexts. His playing and recording credits include the big bands of Stan Kenton, Maynard Ferguson, and Bob Mintzer; groups such as Weather Report, Steps Ahead, Steely Dan, the Yellowjackets, and the London Symphony Orchestra; vocalists Diana Krall, Elvis Costello, Joni Mitchell, Kurt Elling, Pino Daniele, and Kate Bush; and such jazz artists as Chick Corea, Michael Brecker, John Scofield, Freddie Hubbard, Joe Henderson, Kenny Wheeler, John Abercrombie, Eliane Elias, Sadao Watanabe, Gary Burton and Pat Metheny, as well as his own trio. He has appeared in concert as soloist with the Berlin Philharmonic and BBC Symphony Orchestras, Ensemble Modern, and the L.A. Philharmonic New Music Group. Mr. Erskine has recorded 400 albums, including several on his own Fuzzy Music label. Peter conducts clinics, classes and seminars worldwide, teaches at the University of Southern California in Los Angeles and the Royal Academy of Music in London. He was awarded an honorary Doctor of Music degree from the Berklee School of Music, has been the recipient of a *Drum! Magazine* "Drummie" award, the winner of *Modern Drummer Magazine's* Reader's Poll in the Mainstream Jazz category numerous times, and has won a Grammy. Mr. Erskine is a member of the Percussive Arts Society and the International Association of Jazz Educators. Peter plays Yamaha drums, Zildjian cymbals, Evans drumheads, Latin Percussion, Rhythmtech instruments, and Vic Firth mallets, brushes and sticks.

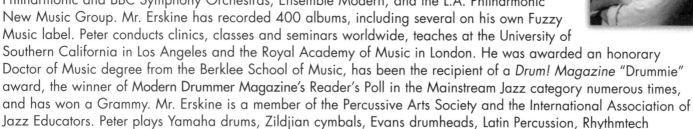

Aaron Serfaty has been playing professionally for 25 years. From 1980–1990 he was the first-call session drummer in his native country of Venezuela. He moved to Los Angeles in 1991 to study jazz, African and Indian music at the California Institute of the Arts. His teachers have included Peter Erskine, Alex Acuña, Joe Cusatis, Albert "Tootie" Heath, Joe LaBarbera, Ignacio Berroa, John Bergamo and Efrain Toro. He co-founded the Cal Arts Latin Jazz Ensemble and co-wrote the Afro-Brazilian/Afro-Cuban Rhythm for Drumset curriculum currently being used at the Los Angeles Music Academy. Mr. Serfaty is also a lecturer at the University of Southern California. His pedagogical activities in Los Angeles include roles as teacher of Afro-Caribbean percussion and its application to the drumset at California Institute of the Arts (CALARTS), co-director of the Latin Ensemble (CALARTS), director of USC's Latin Jazz Ensemble (ALAJE and Latin Jazz Combo), private lessons (USC), instructor of Afro-Caribbean Rhythms for Drumset at Los Angeles Music Academy (LAMA). He has performed, recorded and toured with Brazilian artists Sergio Mendes, Dori Caymmi and Oscar Castro-Neves, and worked with Cuban trumpet virtuoso Arturo Sandoval for 5 years. He recently completed a tour of Japan with Larry Williams and singer Pauline Wilson. Aaron plays Fibes drums, Vic Firth sticks, Zildjian cymbals, and Remo drumheads and percussion.

Acknowledgements

My thanks to all of the good people at Alfred Music for turning this text and music into such a handsome book. Thanks also to my students at USC for their invaluable assistance in this living laboratory of music study I call my teaching studio. Particular appreciation goes to Matt Slocum for his constant enthusiasm and help, in addition to his transcriptions. Co-author Aaron Serfaty's expertise and hard work have ensured that the Afro-Caribbean chapters are comprehensive and authentic. My thanks also to Eric Sokol, who helped me with Finale typesetting in the beginning stages of this book. Special thanks to Ron Davis for so generously loaning me a copy of the now-out-of-print volume *The New Rhythm Book* by Don Ellis, from which I so generously quote. I hope that relaying some of this material will spark additional interest in the music of the late Don Ellis.

My editor, Dave Black, plus his staff, have the experience and work ethic to guarantee that all of the information herein is accurate and user friendly. I should also like to thank every drummer I have listened to and learned from—the list is endless! Finally, my biggest thanks go to my family, who tolerated long absences away from me when I'd lock myself away in my studio to complete this third book in the series that pretty much tells it like it is when it comes to my understanding of drumming.

Thank you!

*I*ntroduction

Welcome to *Drumset Essentials*, Volume 3, and congratulations.

Your reading and studying of the following text and musical examples means you have reached a level of drumming skill and awareness that allows you to freely express yourself in music. I am certain that after successfully completing all three volumes, you will be informed and confident enough to walk into any playing situation and enjoy the experience.

Volume 3 focuses on the following:

1. More advanced brush-playing beats, tips and studies

2. Brazilian and Afro-Caribbean music[1]

3. Metric combinations—possibilities in 4/4 and odd-time (compound) meters

4. General drumming philosophy and work tips (the stuff of 40 years of personal and professional experience), including advanced drumming concepts for approaching fills, solos and "free" music, as well as advice on everyday music business matters

As with the two previous volumes, this book's correlating CD contains play-along tracks without drums as well as complete band tracks with which you can listen to my drumming approaches and style. As always, you are encouraged to listen to as many different drummers and styles of music as possible. "Active listening" is not just simply enjoying the good sounds of some music, but analyzing and growing more and more aware of song form construction, what the other instruments (besides the drums) are doing, plus melodic, harmonic and contrapuntal activity, etc. This is the vital steppingstone that will allow you to connect to and express every kind of music.

Let's continue our study of brush playing from Volume 2 and take it from there—but first, a few more words about the art of **listening**.

Good luck in life and music—and have fun!

Sincerely,

Peter, circa 1962 (8 years old)

> Knowledge is not skill.
> Knowledge plus 10,000 times is skill.
> **—Shinichi Suzuki**

---

[1] I am pleased to welcome colleague and instructor Aaron Serfaty to help teach these classes to you.

Notation Legend

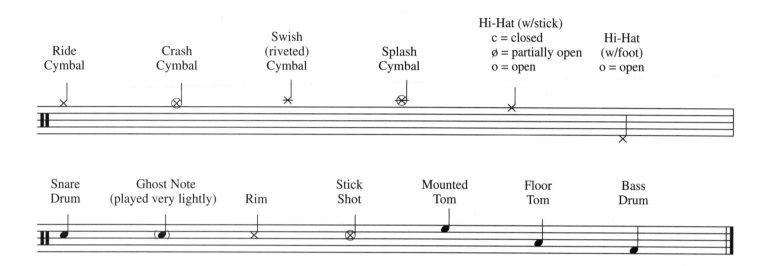

Tempos

Throughout all three volumes of *Drumset Essentials*, students are consistently encouraged to practice the exercises and rhythms at a variety of tempos, notably 60, 90 and 120 bpm. The realm of possible tempos is enormous, and we should be able to play basic jazz and pop styles *anywhere* on the tempo map while keeping a steady beat.

The Importance of Listening

"Listen..."

For all the good advice you'll find from teachers or in books, the greatest instruction about playing music comes from simply **listening** to music. When you ask yourself, what should I play on a particular tune? listen to another drummer's "take" on a song and get some ideas of what to do. Why try to reinvent the wheel on your own when you can learn from countless musical performances that have been recorded? Also, when you listen to music, you should learn song forms. Every time you hear a tune, analyze it and make note of the bar structure in your head. Let's call this *active* listening. I have listened to music all of my life, *passively* as well as *actively*. I enjoy music, and I study music. Like an intellectual who reads as much as possible, a musician who listens is well informed and well rounded.

Assignment No. 1

Listen to as much music and to as many drummers as time will allow.

Assignment No. 2

Record and listen to your own drumming.

Assignment No. 3

With any recording, don't just listen to the drumming, but also pay attention to what **all** the other instruments, including vocals, are doing.

These homework assignments are due every day from now on, for the rest of your life!

My Challenge: Most of us take this sort of listening talent for granted. How do I convey a lifetime's worth of active listening experience to younger ears?

My Solution: Drawing a diagram to help explain my life-long passion for listening made it apparent that there are some concrete and helpful guidelines to offer for both the novice and the experienced listener who want to have a better understanding of what it is that great drummers do. These rules also apply very nicely when we listen to our own recorded performances. As you look at my diagram, please keep in mind that the **first rule of listening** should always be to **ENJOY** the music. Applying some analytical thought and reactive processes to the mix, the following three categories seem to provide a good framework for analysis:

1. Balance

2. Rhythm and Velocity

3. Tone

Balance

Focusing on a drum track, there are two kinds of balance to consider: the *dynamic* balance of the various parts of the kit in relation to one another (as well as in relation to the other instruments playing), and the *textural* balance (which can also be thought of in terms of the *density level* of the various goings-on). The assorted components of the drumset, as well as the beat the drummer is playing, should **balance**, **offset** and **complement** one another.

Rhythm and Velocity

The nature of a drum performance's rhythm can be broken down into these two questions: Is the tempo steady? Does the beat groove? "Yes" or "No" answers will usually suffice. Next, the velocity of the drum track merits our attention. Even if all the previous standards of quality are met, it is worth noting that the ultimate feel or forward motion of the music seems to go round and round in a circle, or it starts and stops (much like a car that starts making progress on the road but then stops and parks, gets moving again, etc.), or that it cruises like a Mercedes on the superhighway.

Tone

Finally, the quality of tone involves the most variables, including *touch* (every drummer's signature), the *sound of the instrument* (sizes of drums, types of heads, choice of cymbals, and even the way the drumset was mic'd and recorded), the *tuning* or *pitch* of the kit, and the *texture* that the drummer achieves. All of these qualities help to give more of a three-dimensional presence to any drum sound.

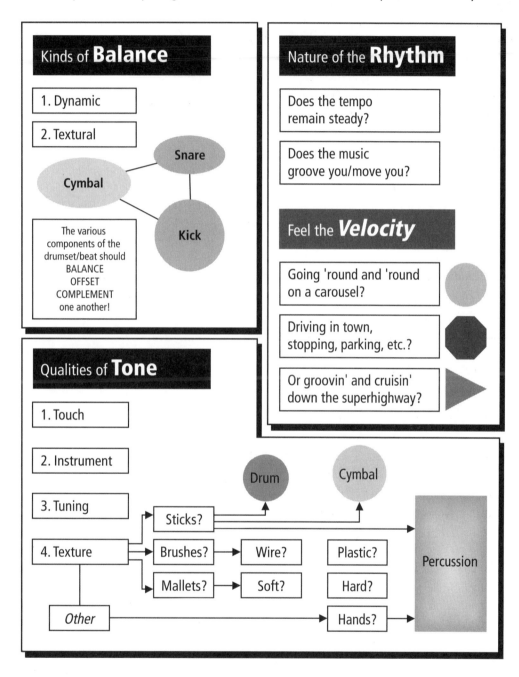

This listening template works not only for drummers listening to drummers, but for other instrumentalists and fans as well. I also advise my students to listen to

   a.   what the other instruments are doing in support of, or reaction to, the drums. This will make the musical reason for the drummer's specific playing choices more apparent;

   b.   their own tracks, **not** as a drummer but as one of the other instrumentalists. How does it feel—how would "you" enjoy accompanying that drum performance? This takes the "you" out of "you," and allows you to see yourself as others might.

A good listener makes for a good drummer.

*B*rushes, Continued

Slow and medium tempos are relatively easy to play when using brushes. The primary characteristics of the sound of brushes on the snare drum should be warm and smooth, relaxed, yet always moving forward, clear and defined, but not brittle or too staccato. *Crisp* is a good adjective that comes to mind. When playing brushes, I like to tell my students to think of Fred Astaire, the great tap dancer whose every move defined elegance. Similar to the technique of a tap dancer, a sweeping brush motion can convey plenty of charm and information, as well as textural sonic nuance. As you try the following sweeping motion examples on the snare drum, follow the direction of the arrows under the notes.

Legato is another word to keep in mind, but be sure that when playing these types of rhythms you are able to achieve some "point" to the beginning of each note (*articulation* means just that, i.e., to be articulate). As always, use your ears to find a proper balance between note articulation and texture.

While Volume 2 of *Drumset Essentials* emphasized the specific technique of *not* using the wrist when using the left-hand brush in a circular pattern on the brush head, it must be stressed that the use of proper **wrist technique** is very important to the execution of brush **rhythms** on the drumhead. The fluid motion created by relaxed wrists in both hands will provide power to the player and the ability to perform any set of rhythmic repetitions with great consistency. Keep the arms loose, shoulders relaxed, and use only as much *overall* motion as is necessary—no more, no less.

REMEMBER: The time is in your **center**, not in your forearms or fingers.

Please note the arrow direction markings for the right and left hands in the following brush exercises. These directions include clockwise swirls, counter-clockwise swirls, and sweeps that go left to right, right to left, and diagonally in both directions across various parts of the drumhead.

Sweeping Exercises

Suggested beginning tempo for these exercises: ♩ = 60 bpm

1.
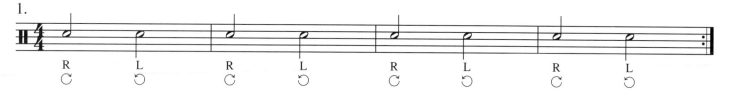

2.
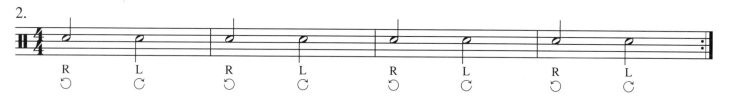

3.

4.

5.

6.

7.

8.

9.

10.

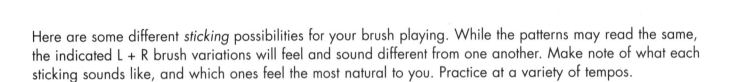

Here are some different *sticking* possibilities for your brush playing. While the patterns may read the same, the indicated L + R brush variations will feel and sound different from one another. Make note of what each sticking sounds like, and which ones feel the most natural to you. Practice at a variety of tempos.

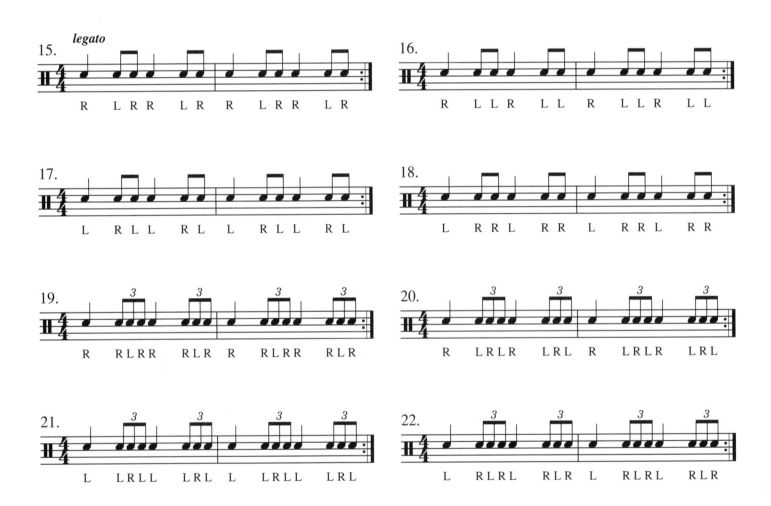

Note: In exercises 23–26, the first three quarter notes of each example should be played with both hands— i.e., a two-handed quarter-note pulse, which is the basic beat for all ballad and medium-tempo brush playing.

Here are some additional end-of-measure transitional rhythms to help familiarize you with phrases that are more dense or take place over a longer period of time than a quarter-note pulse would. Notice that some of the notes will speak with an added emphasis, as if on their own. This is musically natural (accents are the spice of rhythmic life). You can also create additional emphasis by "digging" either brush into the head ("dead stroke") or against the head. This is one of my favorite devices to use when playing brushes.

Try these first at a moderately slow tempo, and then work them up to speed. You should also experiment with different stickings and the placement of these multiple-stroke riffs.

Note: When a brush is finished doing its part of articulating a rhythmic phrase, it should remain on the head and go back into the service of providing a "cushion" of the swirled-pulse sound. This will not only assure the smoothness and continuity of the sound, but the one brush against the head will provide an effective damping or muting effect on the drum by cutting down the open snare drum ring that results from striking an un-muffled drum. This is the technique I use when playing brushes in time. Of course, if you *want* the drum to reverberate or ring, then you should go for that. Know the difference and make your choice, but don't overlook the use of the left hand in damping the drum.

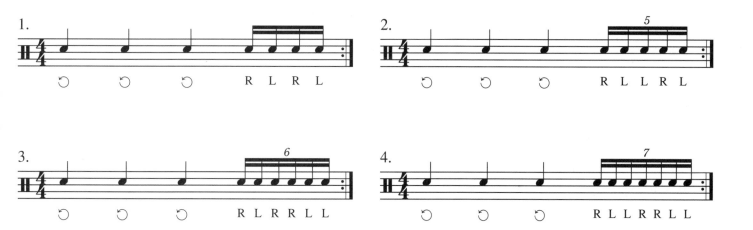

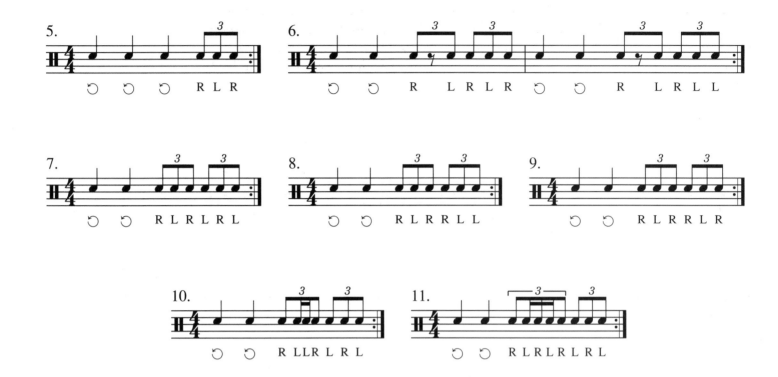

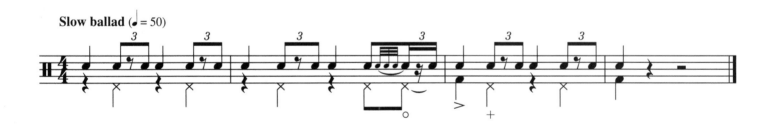

Note: If the pulse or feel of a tune is triplet-based, then you will probably want to avoid playing anything in your time feel, or fills that would suggest a double-time tempo as demonstrated by the following example:

If the tune is based on a slow triplet feel, it's better to keep your connecting phrases in the original "vibe."

Meanwhile, when playing a legitimate double-time feel on a standard tune, (as is done during the *bridge* of a song [A-A-**B**-A]), an option I like to use is to suggest the double-time feel by keeping one of the timekeeping elements in the original (slow) meter. In the following example, the hi-hat stays in the "old" tempo (the "A" part of the form), while the hands play in double time.

Bridge (double-time feel)

Here's another version of the same idea, but this time the hand pattern remains in the old (slow) meter or feel, while the hi-hat doubles up the time:

Bridge (double-time feel)

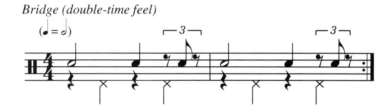

This type of rhythmic awareness and playing will make your music more dimensional.

Using Brushes at Fast Tempos

The very look and sound of brush playing should not evoke the image of perspiration;
however, really fast tempos can make any drummer sweat if they try to play those fast tempos
the "hard way."

Suggested tempo: ♩ = 300 bpm

If you attempt to articulate all of the ride-pattern rhythms with only the right hand at an
extreme tempo such as this (or faster!), a condition similar to that of *rigor mortis* will soon
occur! It makes better sense to break the ride pattern up, or to split it between the two hands:

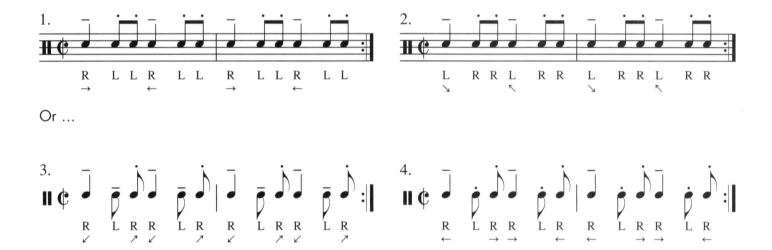

Or ...

In exercise 1, the left hand plays the double-time backbeat. This particular beat is relatively
easy to develop and feel. In exercise 2, the left-hand brush plays the primary (quarter-note)
pulse, while the right hand plays the eighths. It will take some practice to get it from sounding
like the "Lone Ranger" cowboys and horse hooves groove to a swinging rhythm.

Important: The left-hand strokes can alternate back and forth in different directions, as
opposed to making the same brush movement across the head for each and every stroke. Get
the sound you want in your head and then practice it slowly at first, gradually building up
speed. Practice will make perfect, I promise you!

Examples 3 and 4 utilize the same stickings as each other, but with different stroke directions.
"Different strokes for different folks..." Try them, beginning slowly and then working your way
up to speed. Don't be afraid to experiment.

I find that brush playing is an extremely satisfying, but personal, means of self-expression on
the drums. Ultimately, you will want to FIND YOUR OWN WAY.[2] It is worth mentioning that
you owe it to yourself to study and listen to the brush playing of such drummers as Jeff
Hamilton (my favorite brushes player), Elvin Jones, Mel Lewis, Ed Thigpen, Shelly Manne,
Buddy Rich, Louis Bellson, Steve Gadd (for contemporary music, especially), "Papa" Jo Jones,

---

[2] It is worth mentioning that the study of the "art" of brush playing can also include the physical act of "painting" your rhythms on the
drumhead. It is fascinating to watch the brushes sweep across the head in different directions, at varying speeds and angles of attack. This
requires, naturally, that you play with your eyes (and ears) open.

Philly Joe Jones, Don Lamond, Jack DeJohnette, John Riley, Joey Baron, as well as yours truly. You'll not only hear some interesting use of the brushes on the snare drum, but a lot of fascinating interplay between the snare drum and hi-hat, bass drum and cymbals.

Did I forget the tom-toms?

> *Alan Dawson advocated the use of brushes for all sticking and rudimental exercises. He felt by using brushes, one wouldn't be getting much rebound, thereby giving one the sense of "picking up" the sticks. Dawson also stressed proper posture at the drumset and relaxation in body movements, relating these issues to balance in the sound of one's playing and the ability to control all four limbs.*
>
> *I work with brushes a lot. It is a dying art. I started because a pair was thrown in with my first drumset. I thought, "I wonder what these are for?"*
>
> — *Jeff Hamilton*

Well said, Mr. Hamilton.

Your brush playing will benefit from such rudiment-specific practicing as well. Here are some suggestions for brush rudiments on the drumset:

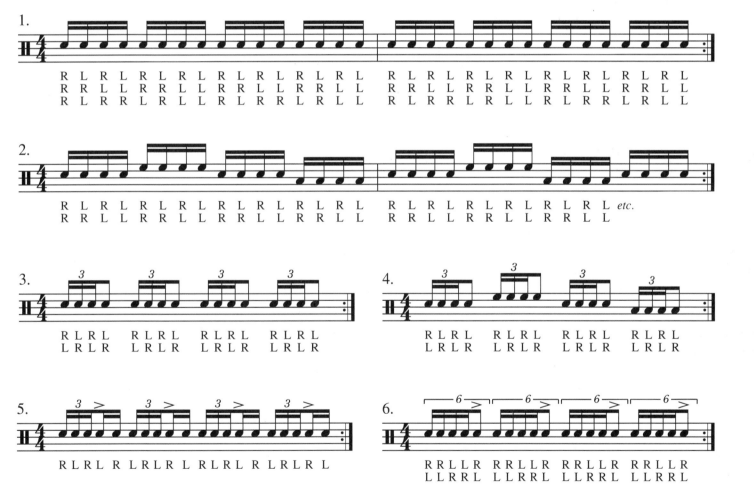

By adding the bass drum to these exercises (and moving the rudiments around the kit), we begin to sound like a real jazz drummer. For additional nuance, use dynamics (such as crescendos) leading up to the accented note. If you have time, a nice effect is to "dead-stick" the brush against the head on an accented stroke.

A multiple-drum sticking variation:

L R R L L R L R R L L R L R R L L R L R R L L R

Additional sticking and multiple-stroke combinations. (You can come up with your own as well, as it is okay to let your hands do some of the thinking.)

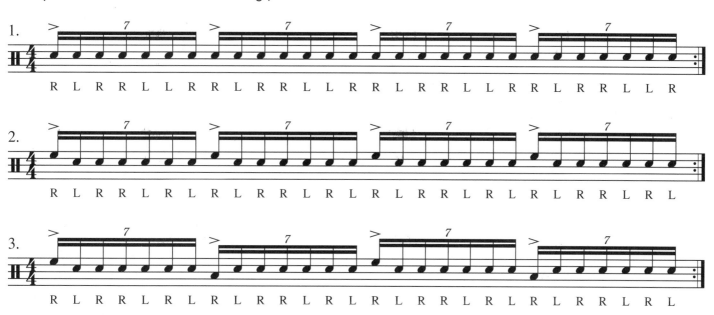

1.

R L R R L L R R L R R L L R R L R R L L R R L R R L L R

2.

R L R R L R L R L R R L R L R L R R L R L R L R R L R L

3.

R L R R L R L R L R R L R L R L R R L R L R L R R L R L

4.

R R L L R R L L R R L L R R L L

You should also practice rudiments such as the flam, drag and ruff while playing brushes. These will add tremendously to your brush-playing vocabulary.

In addition, experiment with non-rudimental techniques, including the one where the brushes are applied to the head and scraped or brushed against the surface in a rapid motion (using the wrists and fingers). This is generally done out of time or tempo, and is a nice textural device that suggests the blowing wind or the fast rustling of leaves. Slower textural strokes against the drumhead can suggest the sounds of flowing water, or someone stretching their legs in a bed with freshly starched sheets! Snowfall. Raindrops. Insects. (?) It's your musical world, so use your imagination!

I also like to play soft "pat" strokes on the snare drum in an arhythmic fashion (i.e., in "free" time) during pauses in a ballad. This produces a fill that has no specific rhythmic reference but is pleasing in its sound quality. (The key is to not play too quickly or emphatically.) Likewise, a few strokes on a cymbal with brushes can provide a lovely color. If your brush has a metal ring at the end of the shaft, you can use that for sound colorations. Additionally, I always have a pair of timpani mallets on hand for soft tom-tom or cymbal rolls to complete a tune's picture.

Finally:

1. Don't spit out the fills, transitional phrases or connective devices you play.

2. Think of the "dance" when you play brushes.

3. Never let 'em hear you sweat.

4. Play "pretty."

5. Always swing.

6. Give 'em something to remember you by... (MUSIC)!

7. A terrific practice tool for the brushes is the Laptop by Rhythmtech. It is a pre-tensioned, coated, 13-inch head with snares attached underneath (extremely portable). I use it for practice as well as for quickie rehearsals when I don't want to bring an entire drumset along.

*B*razilian Drumming

Samba

Keeping our brushes in hand, let's explore the music of our friends south of the border in Brazil. Most of the Brazilian music you'll encounter in playing situations will either be of the samba/bossa nova variety with a steady undercurrent beat in 2, or the *baião* (pronounced BUY-own), which has a syncopated/anticipated Charleston-type bass-drum rhythm and feel.

> *The baião is a very old rhythmic form which may have come from Arab culture. Baião (originally prevalent in the interior region of the country) was introduced to Rio de Janeiro and São Paulo in the 1940s, and its rhythm has since been worked into many styles of music, including jazz and fusion, and, of course, samba where it produced a hybrid known as Samba-Baião... The best known of the many Afro-Brazilian music/dance forms is the samba. The roots of samba are in the Angolan or Congolese dance ... typical samba of today features such elements as 2/4 meter (oft-times with the accent on beat 2), with layers of syncopated rhythms on top...* [3]

First, let's look at the bass drum in 2/4 time where you'll simply play that drum on beats 1 and 2. This is the heartbeat of samba:

You may also play a slight accent on beat 2 with your right foot to suggest or recall the feel of the *surdo* drum (a type of suspended bass drum with a deep sound that is the basic pulse of any samba group).

This is optional, and, in some cases, not necessary (or desirable). Please read on...

It is important to mention that the heel should be in the down or resting position when playing Brazilian musics. The reason is to facilitate the even execution of the rhythms so the player will not overemphasize the on-beat rhythms. Most Brazilian drummers play this way as it helps to ensure that the beats are more equal and consistent; and it is easy to add an accent or emphasis if desired. To be honest, I still go into an up-heel position for up-tempo playing of multiple strokes on the bass drum, and like a tap dancer, I move the toe of my right foot towards the front of the pedal

board when playing multiple strokes. I am careful, however, to "hear" what I want it to sound like and then adjust the dynamic pressure accordingly! My guest author, Aaron Serfaty, recommends that you try to play this music in the heel-down position in order to reduce the movement of mass (in other words, "light is right").

---

[3] From *Brazilian Rhythms for Drumset* by Duduka Da Fonseca/Bob Weiner (Cat. No. MMBK0009CD) © 1991 Manhattan Music, Inc. Used with Permission of Warner Bros. Publications U.S. Inc. All Rights Reserved.

Add the hi-hat on the "ands" of beats 1 and 2:

Since we are playing these examples at a relatively soft volume, I recommend keeping your hi-hat foot's heel in the down position as well when playing this music.

1.

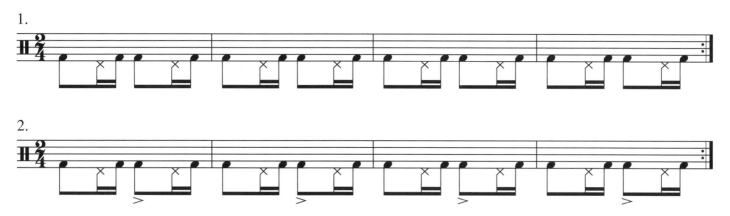

2.

Ultimately, your ear should tell you where the accents should fall in these rhythms.[4]

---

[4] In English, for example, we tend to accent particular syllables such as "Phil-a-DEL-phi-a," or "Hi-ro-SHI-ma," while a Japanese person would pronounce the second city as "Hi-ro-shi-ma," with each syllable receiving equal emphasis. Don't ask me how a Japanese person might pronounce "Philadelphia"!

Drummer Alex Acuña has described the phrasing difference between Brazilian and other musics as follows:

> *If you think of the motion of most music's rhythms as being a ball that is rolling down an incline, then Brazilian music's rhythm is like an egg rolling down that incline...*[5]

Well said. Here is an exercise that will help you to understand and hear this delightful and unique "bump" in Brazilian music. First, play the top line with the right hand and the bottom line with the left, then switch hands!

Play the sixteenth notes in the right hand while you play the eighth-note triplets in the left, and then switch hands! This is an example and manifestation of the uneven nature of most African-influenced music in the Americas.

---

[5] This quote has also been attributed to pianist Don Grusin who has worked with Alex.

We will now add a series of typical and authentic samba rhythms.

First, I would like for you to sing these rhythms (I suggest using the syllable "da") while playing the bass drum as notated. Then, take your brushes and play these rhythms on the snare drum. Experiment with various sticking possibilities such as alternating R-L, adding some double strokes here and there, or playing all of the rhythms with either the left or right hand. How does the phrasing or "feel" change when you use different stickings?

R L R L R R L R   L R L R L R R L

Now, let's add the ride cymbal and hi-hat to this mixture:

Now let's play the dotted eighth and sixteenth-note bass drum beat with the ride cymbal and hi-hat. Please make sure your ride cymbal and bass drum are entirely coordinated when playing *tutti* (unison) rhythms.

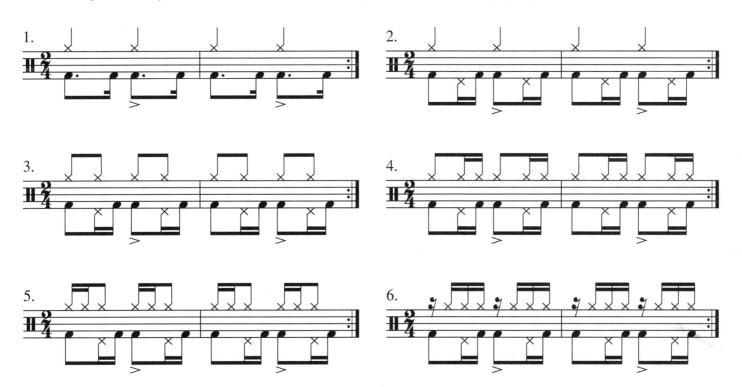

Now, add the left hand, playing the above series of typical and authentic samba rhythms. You should also experiment with orchestrating some of the notes on various parts of the kit. The floor tom will always sound good on beat 2, functioning much like a surdo.

Here's one of my favorite beats. The right hand alternates between the cymbal on beat 1 and the floor tom on beat 2, while the left hand plays the sixteenth-note offbeats. In the first example, the left hand plays all of the offbeats on the snare drum. In the second example, the left hand alternates between the hi-hat and the snare, and the foot (closing the hi-hat on the "ands" of beats 1 and 2) adds shape to the rhythm. With a little practice, you can easily sound like an entire *batucada* or *samba school*. This beat works very well in a variety of samba tunes:

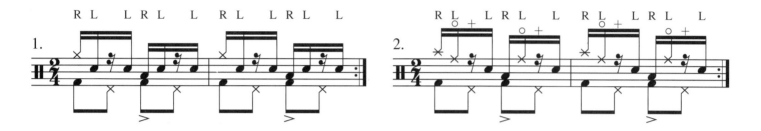

You can experiment with the utilization of all the tom-toms, snare, hi-hat and different cymbals while playing and accenting different sixteenth-note combinations of samba rhythms. Sometimes this can involve the crossing over of your hands on the kit, for example, using the left hand to play the tom-toms while the right hand plays sixteenth notes on the snare. There are some delightful examples of these types of beats that can be found in the *Brazilian Percussion Manual* by Dan Sabanovich (Alfred Publishing Co., Inc.).

Meanwhile, Brazilian drumming (samba) skills will improve from the study and use of such Brazilian percussion instruments as the tamborim.

Tamborim (for musical spacing and phrasing)[6]

The suggested stickings come from the manner in which the tamborim, a small single-headed drum used in samba bands (called *samba schools*), is played. The pattern is notated in the following manner:

Pattern 1 (x = Turn left hand over to meet right stick)

R R (T) R R R (T) R   R R (T) R R R (T) R

The drum is played with a small stick in the right hand. The left hand holds the drum, and the muted tones are controlled with the middle finger pressed against the head. The drum's position is altered for the "x" notes so that on the **upstroke,** the *drum* hits or catches the *stick.*

---

[6] Tamborim photos and examples from *Brazilian Percussion Manual* by Dan Sabanovich (Alfred Publishing Co.)

Another tamborim pattern commonly played in samba is:

Pattern 2

R R(T)R R R(T)R R R(T)R R R(T)R R

Keep the sixteenth note in mind for the feel. Again, the best way to learn the feel or accent to the language of any music is to listen to as much of it as possible. In this case, that would mean recordings or live presentations of Brazilian music. Meanwhile, the use of "trick sticking" or "shortcut sticking" on the drumset will allow you to more easily approximate the real feel of other world musics. Instead of merely alternating the strokes L R L R L R L R, try sticking patterns such as

RRLR   RRLR   RRLR   RRLR

RLLR   RLLR   RLLR   RLLR

with your brushes on the snare drum or sticks on the hi-hat, snare drum, or various parts of the kit, to see how those stickings affect the groove. Such stickings will reflect the feel and sound of the tamborim groove when played on the drumset.[7]

---

[7] For Afro-Cuban drumming, a shortcut sticking can be RLRR RLRR RLRR RLRR. This particular sticking is reminiscent of the right hand execution of the campana or cowbell rhythm (normally played by the bongo player).

Bossa Nova

What is the difference between *samba* and *bossa nova*?

> *The samba is basically a dance form . . . [an] activity engaged in by everyone in Brazil. It is simply a part of the Brazilian culture. . . .*
>
> *The bossa nova is essentially a samba rhythm played in a different way. . . . the bossa style is characterized by its softer and more subtle rhythm. Bossa nova is generally played slower than most sambas...* [8]

Samba was created around and from *percussion*, whereas the bossa nova was created with the drumset solely in mind—it was a piano trio-based music related to the *Choro* or *Chorinho* music of Brazil. Samba is a street music (more or less) with the *cavaquinho*, a Brazilian ukulele, as the primary chordal and melodic instrument.

According to Brazilian guitarist and composer Oscar Castro-Neves:

> Samba is a form of rhythm that encompasses many percussion instruments at the same time. Brazilian guitarist and composer Joao Gilberto (born 1931) decanted the essential array of percussion instruments and rhythms to convey the ESSENTIAL rhythm of samba, making it into a simpler synthesized whole, otherwise known as bossa nova. With the introduction and dissemination of bossa nova, the music of Brazil (samba) became INTERNATIONAL ("local stays local..."). Bossa nova is so reproducible, and the music was understood by so many musicians, that its sound and popularity spread worldwide (and continues today). In samba, there are too many things happening at the same time. Bossa nova is a form of samba, but bossa nova can be so much more minimal. [9]

> *About Joao Gilberto, Miles Davis said, "He could read a newspaper and sound good."*

---

[8] From the *Brazilian Percussion Manual* by Dan Sabanovich (Alfred Publishing Co.).

[9] Oscar Castro-Neves, in a conversation with the author in March of 2003.

In the late1950s, Joao Gilberto began collaborating with the brilliant composer Antonio Carlos Jobim, who was working as an arranger and producer in Rio de Janeiro. Jobim was deeply impressed with Gilberto's songs, and the pair recorded "Bim Bom" and "Chega de Saudade" in July of 1958. The songs met with considerable success, and the pair established the bossa nova sound in Brazil. In 1961, the U.S. State Department organized a good-will jazz tour of Latin America. American guitarist Charlie Byrd immediately became fascinated by Jobim and Gilberto's music, and introduced the music to his friend, soft-toned saxophone genius Stan Getz. Getz later recollected, "I immediately fell in love with it... Charlie Byrd had tried to sell a record of it with I don't know how many companies, and none of 'em wanted it. What they needed was the voice: the horn."

Joao Gilberto   Antonio Carlos Jobim

Getz and Byrd brought the bossa nova sound to the U.S. with their 1962 LP, Jazz Samba, which became immensely popular. It was the 1963 classic "Getz/Gilberto" that made Joao Gilberto an international superstar. The album featured both Jobim and Gilberto, and gave a receptive American audience the first taste of Joao's sophisticated, romantic whisper, Portuguese lyrics and mellow guitar accompaniment. The surprise hit came courtesy of Joao's wife, Astrud Gilberto, for singing the now ubiquitous "The Girl From Ipanema," which was soon an international sensation.[10]

One thing is for certain—you will be using the cross-stick on your snare drum for most of your bossa nova playing. The following suggestion is a matter of personal choice, but I recommend that you first

1. turn your stick around so that the butt end (i.e., the "meatier" part of the stick) will be playing on the rim of the drum;

2. find the "sweet spot" of the stick when playing it on the rim of the snare drum (approximately 1½ to 2 inches from the butt end of the stick);

3. don't grip the stick too tightly (think of it as allowing the stick to vibrate and "sing");

4. let the stick rebound off the rim's edge immediately upon playing. This will produce a much more vibrant sound than if you were to merely leave the stick "dead" against the rim.

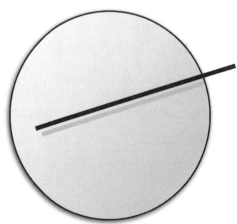

[10] Chung, Christophe, and Joao Gilberto. *The Biography of Joao Gilberto.* Duke University. 20 Apr. 1999. http://www.duke.edu/~msc1/bio.html (1 May 2003).

Turning our attention to the right hand, when playing sixteenth notes on the hi-hat, the phrasing of these notes should not be perfectly even. Let's refer back to the exercise that helps us better understand this delightful and unique "bump" in Brazilian music:

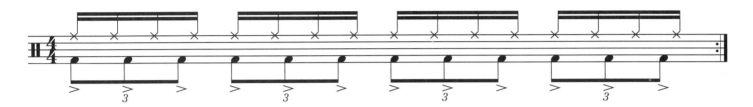

Play the sixteenth notes on the hi-hat while playing the eighth-note triplets with the left hand.

BOSSA NOVA EXAMPLES

Using just the feet:

1.

2.

Now add the hands:

A typical bossa nova pattern:

A reverse bossa nova clave:

A *partido alto* bossa pattern

A partido alto pattern played with brushes on the snare drum:

There are many times I will dispense with the notion of using all four limbs simultaneously when playing a samba or bossa nova, particularly at the beginning of a tune when the dynamics might be soft enough where a fully executed "classic" bossa nova pattern might be difficult to control. In this case, I will usually use two hands on the closed hi-hat, with a soft bass drum on beats 1 and 2 (or only beat 1 or 2 for a while). The stickings can consist of alternating strokes (RLRL), double strokes (RRLL RRLL), or the sticking patterns we explored earlier in this chapter when in the discussion of the tamborim (RRLR RRLR RRLR RRLR and RLLR RLLR RLLR RLLR).

It is also helpful to understand and be able to play the:

Shaker (for rhythmic consistency):

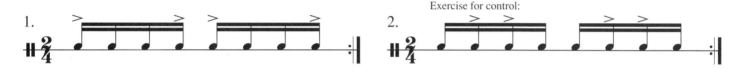

Surdo (for general bass drum feel):

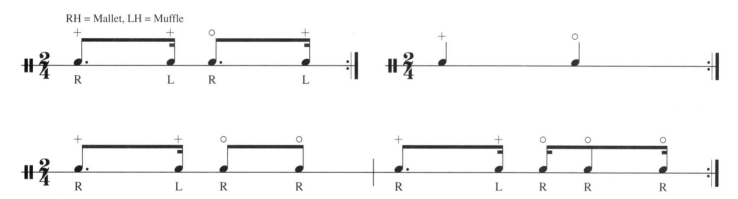

Triangle (for the baião):

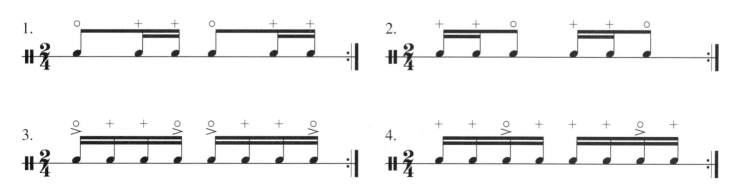

Baião

(for the drumset):

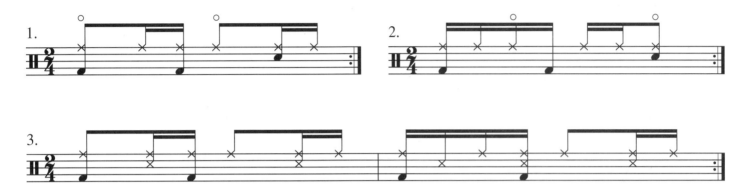

Here's a nice variation of the Brazilian baião beat I came up with during an improvisation that eventually became the Weather Report song "Brown Street" on the album *8:30*. This beat was inspired by a couple of Dom Um Ramao's Afro-Brazilian urban funk grooves, and is actually a combination of two beats I heard on one of Dom Um's recordings. (Rhythm, like life or a restaurant, is a "Blue Plate Combo Special.") Anyway, the best way to learn this rhythm is to start one line at a time. I suggest you begin with the left hand, add the feet, and then play the right hand (snares in the off position). Experiment with the placement of the right-hand stick between the center and rim of the drum. You may also try varying the amount of damping created by the pressure the left hand exerts upon the drumhead. I think you'll enjoy the combination of the right- and left-hand rhythms.

The drumset can sound like an entire percussion section with this one:

BROWN STREET

By Josef Zawinul/Wayne Shorter

While the bass drum and cross-stick pattern was easily evident in Dom Um's playing, the snare drum/right-hand "melody" was inspired by what the rest of the band was playing on that recording. I find I get many drumming ideas from hearing what the rest of the rhythm section is playing, or from what a horn player or vocalist is doing. In Brazilian music, one of the best resources for ideas, inspiration and feel comes from listening to what the (acoustic) guitarists are playing in samba and bossa nova.

Another suggestion: While the cross-stick plays variations of patterns in most samba and bossa nova musics, you should also think of the cross-stick as a possible (and effective) counterpoint to a melody or improvisation that is occurring. If not over-used, an occasional run of three, four or five cross-stick notes (eighths in 4/4, sixteenths in 2/4) makes for a nice percussive effect.

BRUSH AND STICK COMBINATION

Going back to Samba-Land, here's a beat that was inspired by (and pretty much copied from) the ever-tasteful drummer Grady Tate. The right hand plays with a brush while the left hand plays cross-stick on the snare drum (with occasional beats on the small tom). The brush plays a form of the guiro pattern on the snare (relaxation and "snap" are the keys to getting this to sound just right).[11] The combination of the two sound elements produced with a stick and brush is elegant and sure to get a smile from the band. I've recorded this on a couple of Kurt Weill tunes: "My Ship," from my first solo album, *Peter Erskine*, and "Speak Low" on *Sweet Soul*.

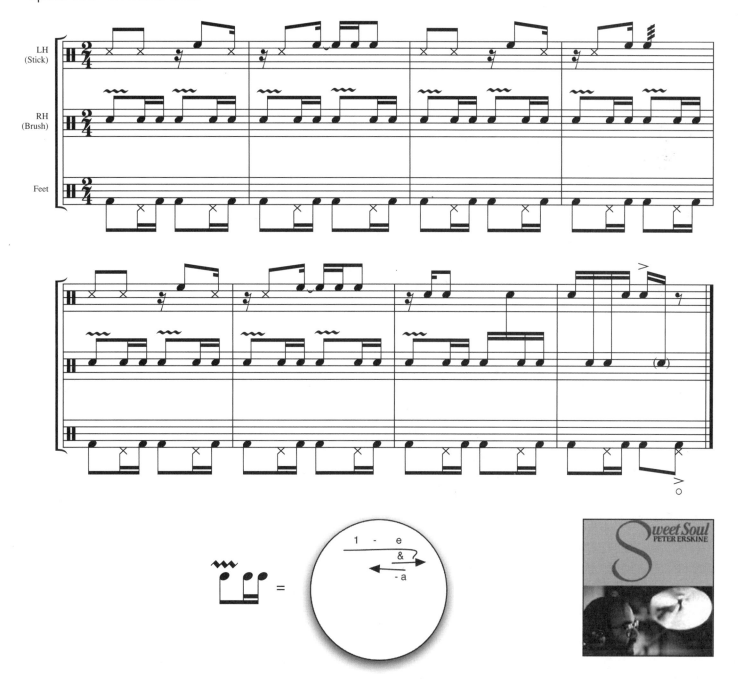

---

[11] In addition to the pattern of movement suggested on this page, you can also try the playing motion-pattern of the guiro with the right-hand brush on the snare head. Let your ears be your final guide. If you can make it sound good with just one hand alone, then you know you're in business.

Recommended for Further Study

Brazilian Rhythms for the Drumset by Duduka Da Fonseca/Bob Weiner

Brazilian Percussion Manual by Dan Sabanovich (Alfred Publishing Co.)

Inside the Brazilian Rhythm Section by Nelson Faira and Cliff Korman

I now introduce you to your instructor for the next chapter, Señor Aaron Serfaty.

Afro-Carribean Drumming

To play Afro-Cuban (or Brazilian) music authentically, it is necessary to be able to recognize the patterns and roles of the traditional percussion instruments and their feel, and realize that that is the "meat and potatoes" of this particular music. Then, we need to apply those patterns to the drumset, which is a challenge in terms of coordination and sound (a 14-inch tom-tom doesn't sound at all like a conga, for example).

In Afro-Cuban music, the main protagonist is the **conga** drum. Originally, the conga was only used for rumba and other styles of mostly African music, but managed to make its way into *son montuno*, *guaracha*, *cha-cha*, *mozambique* and *songo*, among others. These styles are also collectively known as *salsa*.

The **bongo** was the first and, for a while, only percussion instrument in Afro-Cuban music, specifically *son*. It is the timekeeper and also improvises and interacts in a call-and-response manner with the lead instrument or vocals during the verses of songs. During the refrains of songs, the player stops playing the bongos and starts playing a cowbell called *campana* ("bell" in Spanish). Understanding this particular pattern and its feel is of paramount importance in our studies.

Last but not least are the **timbales**. A direct descendant of the timpani family (*timbal* is the French word for "timpani"), they add drive and color to the music with three distinct sound sources: The drumheads, the *cascara* ("shell" in Spanish), and the cowbells. Each of these sound sources has its function according to the style and section of the music.

We have a variety of options that can be used to substitute for the traditional instruments in terms of sound. The hi-hat or the side of a floor tom can be used instead of the cascara. A small tom-tom can be used in place of a conga, and a snare drum (with the snares off) can be used to simulate the timbales. The bongo pattern can't be imitated easily, so we will concentrate on the campana, which can be imitated by a ride cymbal. Better yet, a cowbell can be added to our drumset and incorporated into other styles of music without breaking the bank or our backs. All of this information is very important to know so we can be flexible in a variety of situations (such as playing in a salsa or Latin jazz band with one, two, three or no players.).

The other major consideration is the feel of the music. In order for us to be able to play with the correct feel, we have to understand the polyrhythmic quality that this music inherited from its African predecessor. Once this has been achieved, we must listen to it as much as possible, play along with the recordings and, if possible, learn the dance steps.

As a side note, I strongly believe that one's place of birth is absolutely irrelevant when it comes to learning this or any other kind of music. If we are dedicated and serious enough, we will be able to play it with conviction and authority. In other words, "nurture" is more important than "nature."

Lesson 1: The Feel of Afro-Caribbean Music

The first thing we need to do is familiarize ourselves with the feel of the music. Most teachers will tell you to listen to the music, and that is definitely the way to do it; however, very few will tell you what you are listening for. The main character of Afro-Cuban music is the juxtaposition of a strong 3 over 4. This gives the subdivision of the music a gray-area quality (neither straight eighths nor triplets) that is a direct consequence of its African roots.

I have devised some exercises for your hands that will allow you to recognize what we are looking for. These exercises can be played with your hands on your thighs or with sticks on the drumset. Practice each one individually, and then play them as one continuous exercise with each line repeated four times, then twice, and finally one time.[12] After you've become comfortable, try playing them in an "X" fashion (first bar of line 1, second bar of line 2, second bar of line 1, first bar of line 2). The goal is to phrase the lead hand (the right) the same way each time.

The next step is to turn them into a drumset exercise by adding the hi-hat with the foot and the bass drum. With the right hand, play on the side of the floor tom (cascara effect), the ride cymbal cup, or a cowbell. Follow the same practice routine as above. The goal is to be able to phrase your lead hand (clave) the same way, regardless of the subdivision played in the other hand.

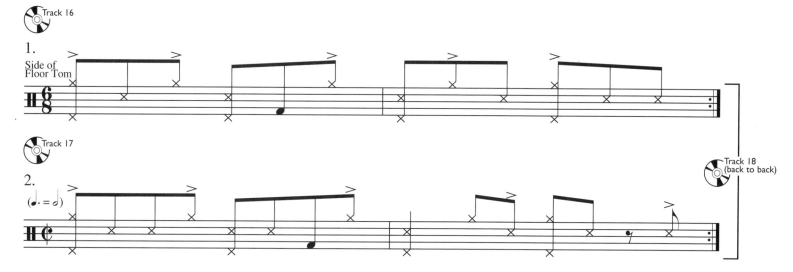

This is the first step to understanding the feel of this music. Now we can go back and listen to our Afro-Cuban music collection with a different set of ears.

---

[12] The indication ♩. = ♩ means that the pulse of the new tempo's half note will equal the value or the speed of the old tempo's dotted quarter note. This device is common in music where metric modulations or precise tempo changes are desired.

Lesson 2: Playing in Clave

Now that we know how the music feels, we need to understand the concept of playing *in clave.*

Clave can be defined as the rhythmic **key** to a particular style of music.[13] All music has its own clave, though not necessarily the Afro-Cuban one (there is a rhythmic key to every type of music). In our case, there is a "tension and release" quality inherent to the Afro-Cuban pattern itself. A common way of describing it uses the concept of a *strong* side (the "3" side), and a *weak* side (the "2" side). The strong side has a downbeat as part of the pattern; the weak side does not. The rhythmic patterns we play will compensate for this by playing downbeat-oriented figures on the weak side, and most syncopated figures on the strong side.[14] This determines the direction of the music in relationship to the clave (3-2 or 2-3).

Note: In *traditional* Afro-Cuban music, once a direction is established, *it will not change.* In modern Afro-Cuban music, however, rules are sometimes bent but not completely broken. For example, there may be a one-bar rest in an arrangement followed by a section of music that will start in the same clave as before (disregarding the previous direction of 2-3, followed by a bar of rest, then 2-3). A good example that comes to mind is music of the amazing group Irakere.

"2-3 or 3-2?"

This is the number-one question for most drummers who are not very familiar with this music. Here are a couple of key listening points:

1. You should be able to discern the direction of the clave from the melody. Please refer to "Manny's Setup," **Track 12** on the *Drumset Essentials 3* CD, for a demonstration. This tune, composed and played by pianist Otmaro Ruiz, has a spoken tutorial by Aaron Serfaty that demonstrates the "how" to figuring out the clave of a piece of music.

2. The timbal pattern will give you the direction of the clave (i.e., 2-3 or 3-2) if you just listen to the rhythm of the cascara. The conga pattern can also provide a clue. Please note the "2" and "3" number indications in the following examples.

---

[13] *Clave* is the Spanish word for "clue." The word itself comes from the Latin *clavis*, which means "key."

[14] For example, in a piano *montuno* (vamp two-bar pattern) the bar with the downbeat in the piano would be the "2" side of the clave, or the clave side where a downbeat is NOT played.

Lesson 3: Salsa

Son, son montuno, and *guaracha* patterns (collectively known as *salsa*) are applied here to
the congas, bongo, timbal and drumset.[15]

These styles are usually played to son clave:

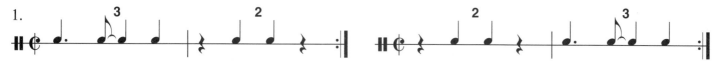

A basic conga *marcha* pattern (used for verses and piano solos):

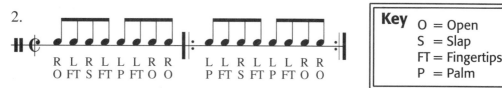

Key
O = Open
S = Slap
FT = Fingertips
P = Palm

A basic conga *mambo* pattern (used for refrains):

A basic timbal *cascara* pattern (used for verses and piano solos):

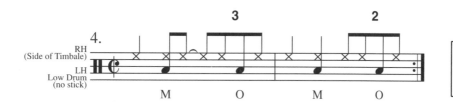

Key
M = Mute
O = Open

Used for refrains:

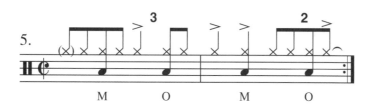

---

[15] For Afro-Cuban drumming skills, the student will benefit from being able to play the following percussion instruments: conga, timbales, and
bongo/campana. If you are a student at a university and your school offers instruction in these instruments, you are encouraged to take up the study
of them. Similarly, you should seek instruction from any local music shop or percussionist whose playing you've heard, appreciated or admired
(whether or not the player is a competent instructor might be a different story). Even without utilizing the ability to play these instruments, you
should look at the patterns in this chapter to get an idea of what these instruments do in a typical Afro-Cuban music setting. Compare what you see to
what you hear when you listen to this music.

A basic bongo *martillo* pattern (used for verses):

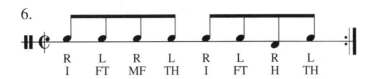

Campana (played by the bongo player and used for refrains):

Drumset application without percussionists:

Mambo (used for refrains):

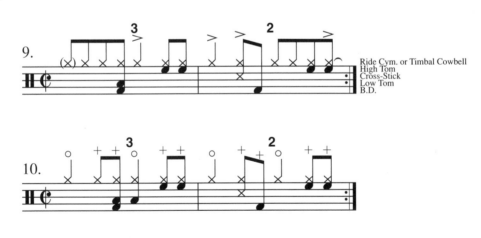

Key   o = Cup of Ride Cymbal or Cowbell
+ = Body of Cymbal

With conga player (used for verses):

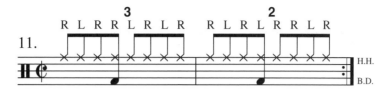

Keeping the above hi-hat pattern, use the following bass drum variations:

All the bass drum patterns are applicable to these patterns.
Drumset application with conga, bongo and timbal:

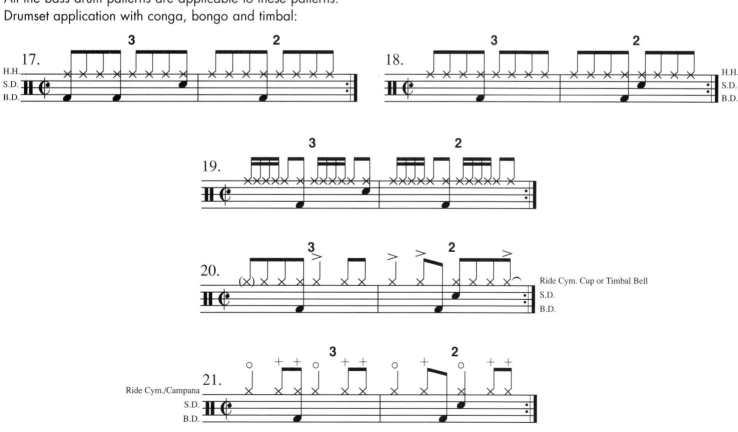

Drumset application with conga and bongo player (used for verses):

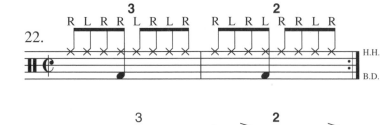

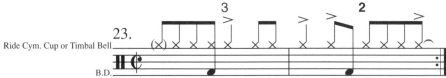

I almost always put the backbeat on the "2" side on beat 3 to help ground the weak side of the clave.

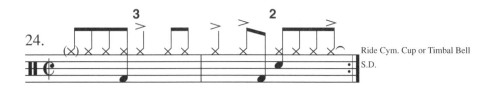

Drumset application with conga, bongo and timbal players (used for verses):

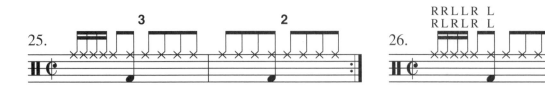

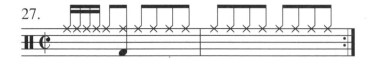

Lesson 4: Cha-Cha

The most relevant instruments in cha-cha are the timbal and the güiro. They provide the drive and the sonic signature of the style. The timbal is described in the salsa lesson. The *güiro* is a gourd with grooves carved out in a horizontal manner. To make it sound, scrape it with a wooden stick in an up and down motion. A plastic version of this instrument is also available; it works exactly the same way as its natural counterpart, but is louder.

The conga is also very important, as it plays the basic marcha pattern. To give you an idea of how they work together, listen to the most famous cha-cha, "Oye Como Va," by the late, great Tito Puente (this song was popularized by Carlos Santana).

For drumset application, we will use the cross-stick as a substitute for the cha-cha bell (small, high-pitched, dry), and the hi-hat as a substitute for the güiro.

Here are the basic patterns for the timbal and guiro as applied to the drumset:

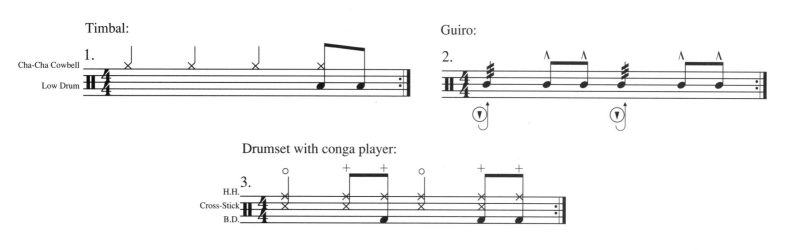

Timbal:

Guiro:

Drumset with conga player:

Drumset with conga player and guiro:

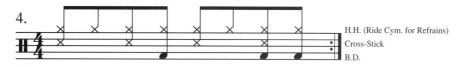

Drumset with conga player, guiro and timbale:

Drumset without percussion:

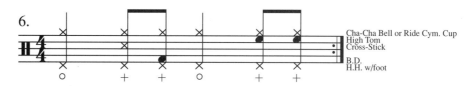

Drumset without percussion:

Lesson 5: Merengue

Merengue is the most popular style of music to come out of the Dominican Republic. The main percussion instruments (in traditional settings) are the *tambora*, a double-headed drum about 12-by-12 inches that is played sideways on the lap, with a stick in the lead hand and the other hand open, and the *güira*, which is a metal version of the güiro. In most modern bands, congas have also been added to the ensemble to complement the tambora. Because of the similarities in sound and function, the congas can be used to substitute for the tambora.

As with the Afro-Cuban patterns, it is important to know the patterns of each of these instruments so we can play merengue with conviction and authority. Again, when we play merengue on the drumset, we need to be aware of the instrumentation (tambora? güira? congas?) of the ensemble so we can play accordingly.

Below are the basic patterns of the tambora, the güira, and the congas and their application to the drumset. Again, the goal is to approximate the sounds as much as possible using every part of the drumset—the snare drum (with the snares off), the side of the floor tom, the rims, etc.

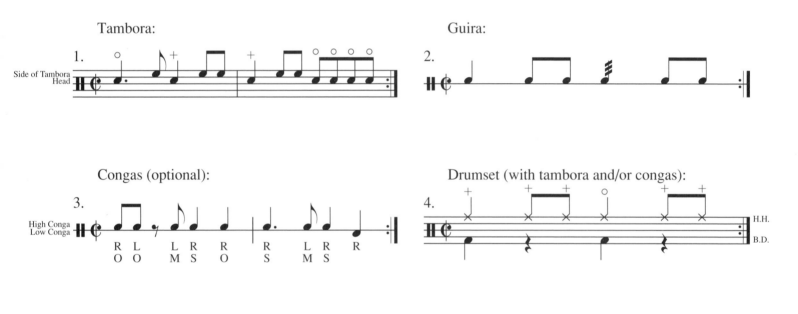

Tambora:

Guira:

Congas (optional):

Drumset (with tambora and/or congas):

With guira only:

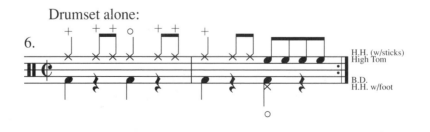

Drumset alone:

Lesson 6: Calypso

Calypso is a very popular Caribbean style of music that originated in Trinidad and Tobago (off the eastern coast of Venezuela). It is played during the Carnaval, and its main characteristic is the use of steel drums and/or steel pans, which provide both the melody and harmony. Harry Belafonte popularized calypso in the United States, and Sonny Rollins wrote "St. Thomas," a calypso that has become a standard in the jazz world.

Here are some calypso patterns as applied to the drumset:

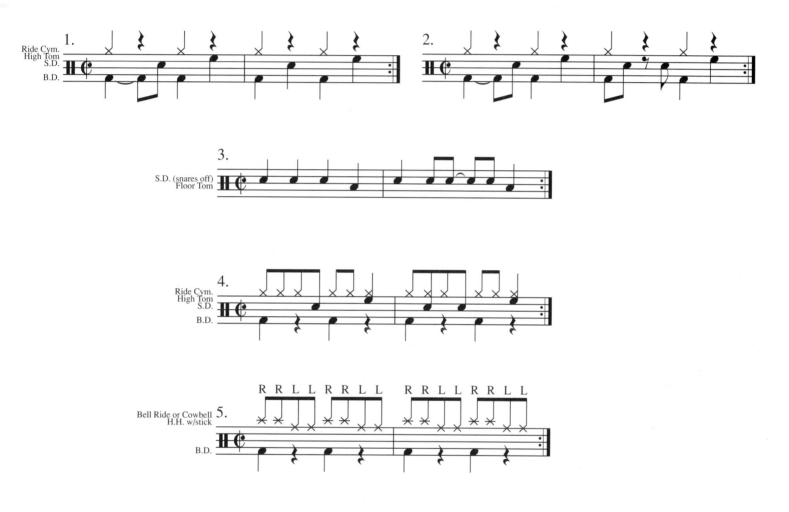

*   *   *

The exciting big-band Latin chart on the following page was composed and arranged by Gordon Goodwin for his Big Phat Band. The performance track features Wayne Bergeron on trumpet and Luis Conte on percussion. The tune's clever title pays homage to the late, great Tito Puente, famed timbalist and bandleader.

The drum part, again from the recording session, gives plenty of information about the band's hits and drum fills, etc. The new tempo at measure 84 is clearly heard in the piano *montuno* figure (a repeated syncopated vamp played by the piano). The written fill in the last measure suggested more of a samba feel than a mambo, so I took the liberty of changing it to a run of sixteenth notes! Please note that there is no click or count-off for this play-along track; the tune starts with Luis Conte's conga drumming. You are invited to "come in" when you like!

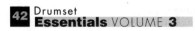

Drums

In memorium Tito Puente

Horn of Puente

WRITTEN FOR WAYNE BERGERON

Track 2 (w/drums)
Track 8 (w/o drums)

COMPOSED & ARRANGED BY
GORDON GOODWIN (ASCAP)

-5-

The importance of knowing Afro-Cuban rhythms and their application to the drumset cannot be stressed enough. Even if you don't get the opportunity to play in a Latin jazz or salsa band, you will be able to use these and other patterns to enhance whatever kind of music you play. A great example of this is the track "Acknowledgement," from John Coltrane's *A Love Supreme* (quite possibly **the** quintessential jazz album, recorded in 1964), in which Elvin Jones begins the tune by playing old-style, traditional mambo and then transitions into a mozambique.

The next patterns were the hip Latin patterns of the day.

Recommended for Further Study

Books

Afro-Cuban Rhythms for Drumset by Frank Malabe and Bob Weiner (Warner Brothers Publications, 1994), book and CD.

The Essence of Afro-Cuban Percussion and Drum Set by Ed Uribe (Warner Brothers Publications, 1996), book and CD.

Understanding Latin Rhythms by Norbert Goldberg (Latin Percussion, Inc., 1973, Warner Brothers Publications, 2000), book and two CDs, LPV110CD.

For your Rhythm Section

The Salsa Guidebook by Rebeca Mauleon (Sher Music Company, 1993).

The Salsa Guidebook is 260 pages filled with musical examples for piano, bass, drumset and salsa percussion instruments. Also included are excerpts of musical scores showing how each instrument fits into each variation of salsa, an historical synopsis, numerous photos of salsa artists and an extensive discography of Afro-Caribbean music. For beginning to advanced players.

Videos

Giovanni Hidalgo: In The Tradition featuring Giovanni Hidalgo (DCI Music Video, Warner Brothers Publications, 2000), VHS with booklet.

In the Tradition, featuring Giovanni Hidalgo, is a master class on traditional conga rhythms and techniques. Giovanni is accompanied by other musicians and explains basic conga playing techniques. A 32-page instructional booklet is included.

Close-Up on Bongos and Timbales by Richie Gajate-Garcia (Latin Percussion, Inc., Warner Brothers Publications, 2002) VHS.

In addition to exercises, this features a full salsa band, including Luis Conte on congas, performing three songs you can play along with.

Thank you, Aaron. Now I would like to discuss...

Odd Meter Subdivisions

Grouping in 2s and 3s

Most of the music I have encountered in my drumming life has been in 4/4 meter. As discussed earlier, samba is traditionally felt and notated in *binary* (2/4) time.[16] The waltz, in 3/4 time, has three beats per measure and is familiar to most everyone.[17]

In a jazz waltz, the drummer has the choice of playing the following:

1. The classic "ting-ting-a-ting" ride pattern:

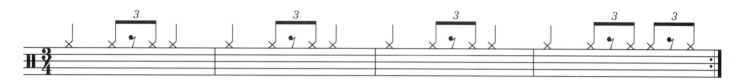

2. The same ride pattern with the hi-hat on beats 2 and 3:

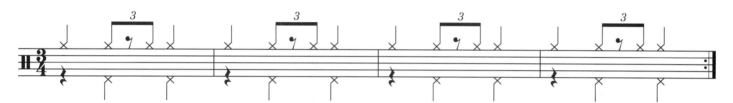

3. The same ride pattern with the hi-hat on all three beats:

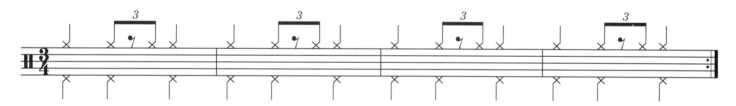

4. The ride pattern with the bass drum playing dotted quarter notes, a *duple* feel:

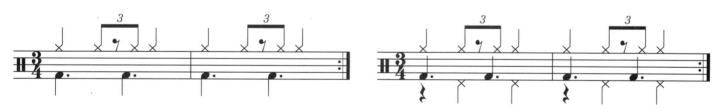

---

[16] Prior to the mid 1950s, almost all jazz was in duple meter (with two or four beats to the bar); the built-in steadiness of such a pulse allowed for the development and use of a variety of syncopation, anticipation and hemiola rhythmic devices, especially during the swing and be-bop eras.

[17] The use of 3/4 in jazz was a novelty at first, notably introduced in 1942 by Fats Waller in his composition "Jitterbug Waltz." Max Roach and Sonny Rollins followed suit in the 1950s by incorporating 3/4, 6/4 and 6/8 into their compositions. Today, jazz music is played in any number of metric settings and most of us are pretty used to it. This was not the case in the early 1960s, when leading jazz educator John Mehegan declared that anything not in 4/4 couldn't be considered jazz! Dave Brubeck, Stan Kenton and Don Ellis changed *that*. Dave Holland's music continues the good fight today.

5. Adding the hi-hat, and extending the ride pattern a bit:

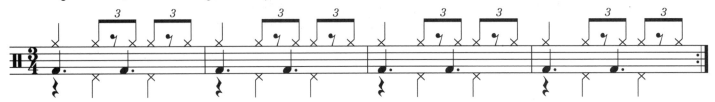

6. A straight-ahead "walking" 3:

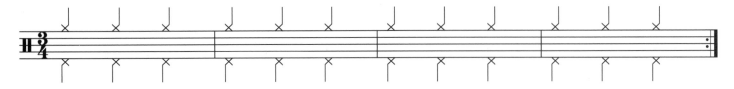

7. The bass drum and snare playing offset duple beats, the classic example of a *hemiola.* This type of approach can be employed quite effectively in 4/4 time as well (the snare and bass drum patterns will cross over the bar line in that case. Instant Elvin Jones!).

In 3/4 time:

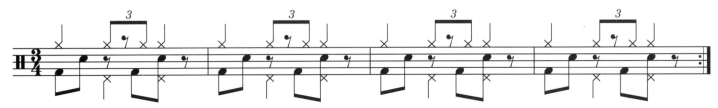

or this variation:

In 4/4 time (Swung eighth-note ride, with hi-hat on 2 & 4):

Elvin-ish 3/4 Grooves

PLAYED BY
PETER ERSKINE

TRANSCRIBED BY
MATT SLOCUM

Because most of us have repeatedly heard music in 3/4 time ("Happy Birthday," "My Country 'Tis of Thee," the waltzes of Johann Strauss, etc.), it seems second nature to play in 3/4 time and always know where we are in each measure of music. The same, of course, also goes for music in 2/4 and 4/4 time. We can do interesting things rhythmically **within** a bar of music, or "over the bar line," and through two or more measures of music (without playing beat 1 of each passing measure), by means of syncopation, hemiola and accented sub-groupings.

All of the rhythms we've explored in this volume have been expressions of "2s and 3s"—in other words, rhythms made up of note values that are subdivided in groups of two or three. Perhaps without even realizing it, you have played many complex patterns of two- and three-note combinations. A good exercise to specifically strengthen your knowledge and gestalt[18] of where beat 1 is at all times is to play the following rhythmic groupings in 4/4 time. (A metronome with an accent-on-beat-1 option is a good thing to have for this exercise.) These first examples are relatively simple and straightforward.

You can play any one of the notes on any part of the kit!

Another way to think of these types of rhythmic conundrums is to sub-group the larger groups of 5, 7, 9, etc., into smaller subdivisions of 2s and 3s.

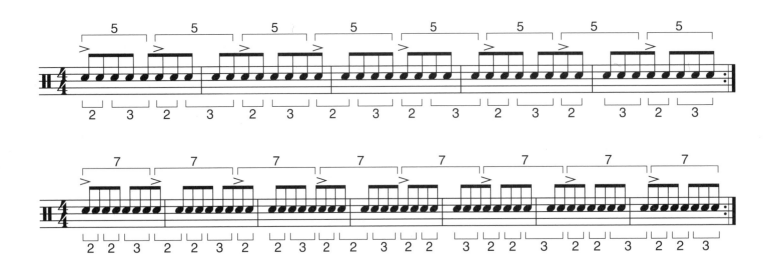

---

[18] Perceptual awareness of structure and space.

These types of odd and even rhythmic groupings in 4/4 are not only the life blood of syncopated swing, they also suggest world music references. Some of these rhythms will sound familiar if you were paying attention to the samba and bossa nova chapter, or if you have listened to music from India or the African continent. They may also suggest sophisticated and complex contemporary music that has yet to be named—although Tony Williams brought such complexities into the world of jazz drumming back in the early 1960s with examples like these:

Tony Williams' rhythmic subdivisions on "Walkin'"—near end of the tenor solo (from *Miles Davis in Europe*)

Twenty years ago, I borrowed this device to figure out a drum part for the introduction of a new tune that we were working on back in the days of the Steps Ahead band. Composer Mike Mainieri didn't want me to play something with just a back beat on 2 and 4, so I came up with the next obvious thing. (This song is on the album *Modern Times*, one of my favorites.)

OOPS (INTRO/DRUM PART)

MIKE MAINIERI

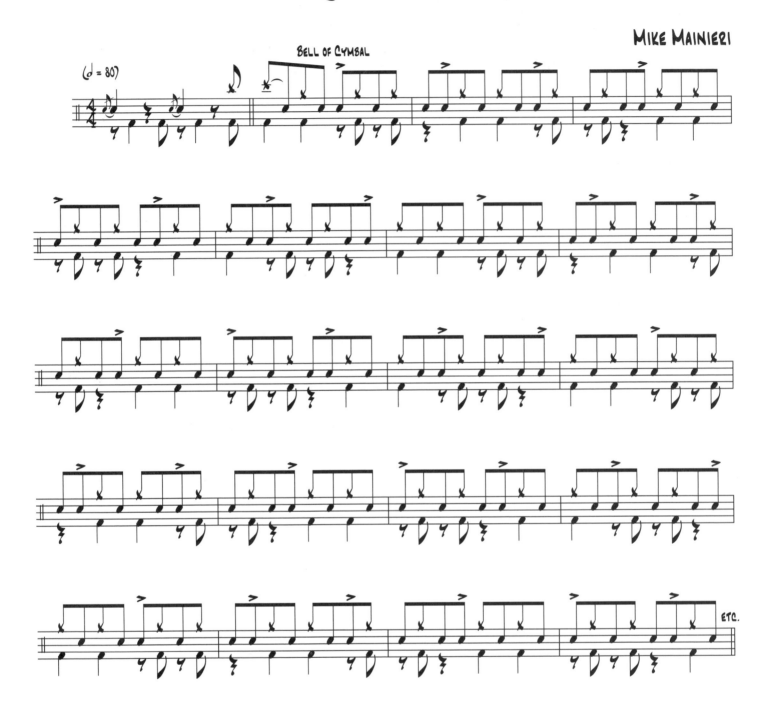

Here is a fascinating rhythmic example. Taking the subdivision 3-3-2 with an accent at the beginning of each group, you'll notice that the phrase sounds very much like the Brazilian baião:

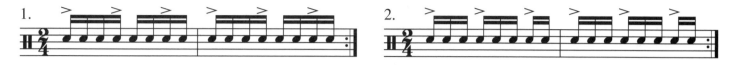

Now, instead of treating this rhythm in duple fashion, let's have some fun and utilize the grouping as a series of accented eighth-note triplets in 4/4 time:

Tricky!

Ravi Shankar, the famed Indian musician, composer and master of the sitar, showed that devilishly clever rhythmic cycle to odd-meter pioneer Don Ellis.

Here is that same rhythm with more visual clues and explanatory tuplet markings:

Okay—before we proceed any further, let's play a simple and delightful waltz for piano trio. This lovely tune, penned by bassist Dave Carpenter, is in the bona fide time signature of 3/4 (and not superimposed on top of something else). On the performance track from my trio's *Badlands* CD (Fuzzy Music), I begin the tune on brushes and later switch over to sticks. You may play it with brushes, sticks or both; for practice, you can play with brushes throughout. Simplicity and openness are the key elements here, in addition to playing lightly and with a sense of swing. The chart provided here is the piano lead sheet I read at the recording session. Have fun and be musical.

Here's a basic drum beat in 3/4 time:

Summer's Waltz

Track 1 (w/drums)
Track 7 (w/o drums)

Dave Carpenter

12/8 Time

Since we've been working in 4/4 and 3/4 meter, it would be a good time now to investigate the most versatile of compound meters: 12/8.

In many world musics, 12/8 is a primary metric template. I would like to show you some subdivisions that appear in African drumming. A bell pattern common in many musics from the African continent (particularly from the country of Ghana) looks like this:

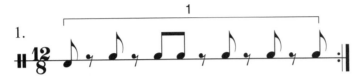

This bell pattern should sound familiar to you by now, as it's the same rhythm we explored that was written in 6/8 at the beginning of the Afro-Caribbean section. You may or may not realize that most of the drumming we enjoy playing and listening to originally comes from Africa.

Here is that same bell pattern subdivided in various possible groupings. Play the bell pattern with one hand while saying or tapping out the rhythmic sub-grouping.

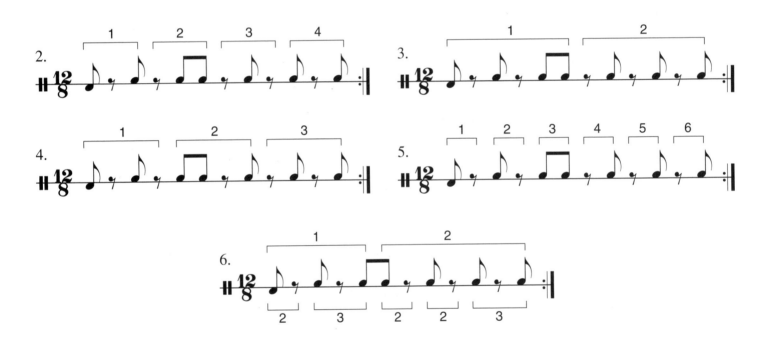

Isn't it interesting how the same rhythm can feel so different just by the natural emphasis that comes from each subdivision and grouping of notes? It should be noted that in traditional African dance, the dancers prefer the grouping where the pattern is subdivided into four equal accents or parts. While examples 1 through 5 were all divided equally (notes in groups of two, three, four, etc.), example 6 breaks the same-sounding phrase into an apparently complex combination of 5/8 and 7/8, subdivided 2-3 2-2-3.

If this is beginning to sound Greek to you, then good, because that's where we're going...

Odd Time

5/4 Time

 19 The Dave Brubeck Quartet recording of Paul Desmond's composition "Take Five" changed modern music for good in the early 1960s:

As you can see, the song is built around a 5/4 pattern that basically equals one bar of 3/4 plus one bar of 2/4 (i.e., a measure feels like a jazz waltz plus two beats).

Joe Morello's melodic, technically perfect, and rhythmically challenging solo changed **me** for good. Morello, thanks to his innate musicianship, intelligence, and practice (the band probably woodshedded the odd-time meter music fairly religiously) enabled him to go from this...

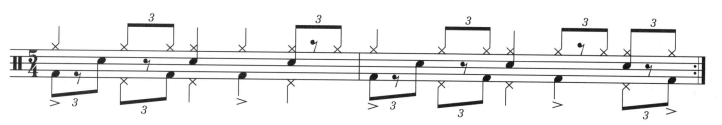

...to all sorts of variations, both in his timekeeping as well as his extended solo. Familiarity breeds a musical comfort zone, as well as the ability to play several bars of 5/4 or 7/8 or 33/16 without having the need to play "1" on the downbeat of each bar with the bass drum! Actually, I suspect Mr. Morello had a natural gift for polyrhythms and this type of music.

2 + 3 = 5

Basic math teaches us that 3 + 2 also equals 5, and so does 1 + 1 + 1 + 1 + 1.

Likewise, you can play 5/4 as:

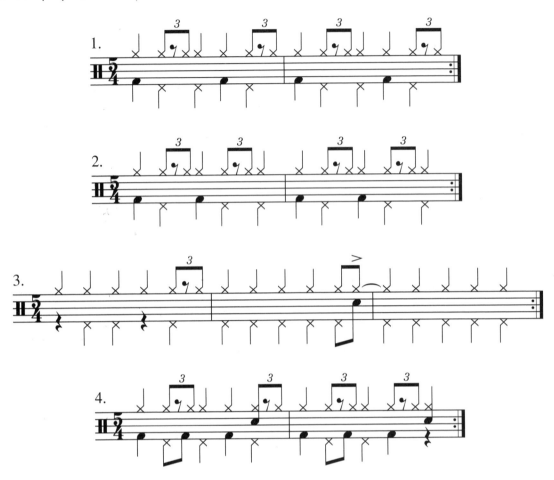

The three-pulse part of the measure can be played in the following ways:

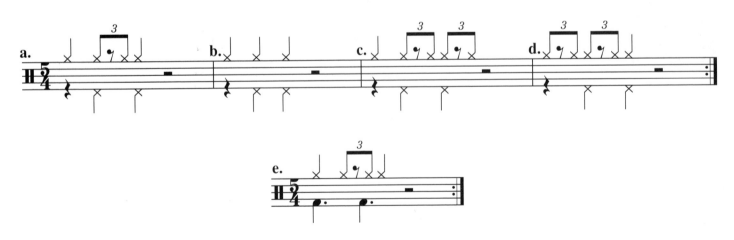

a. ting-ting-a-ting
b. ting-ting-ting (walk)
c. 1 + 2 subdivision
d. 2 + 1 subdivision
e. dupled (turned into two dotted quarter notes)

When playing odd-time meters in most jazz music, the three-pulse part of the bar will often be dupled while the two-pulse part will be walked.

$2 + 2 + 3 = 7$

1.
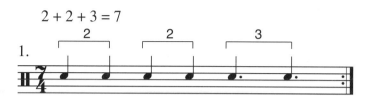

$3 + 2 + 2 = 7$

2.
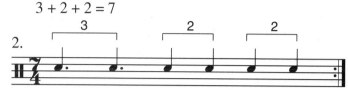

$2 + 3 + 2 = 7$

3.
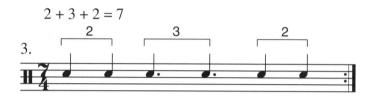

$2 + 2 + 2 + 3 = 9$

4.
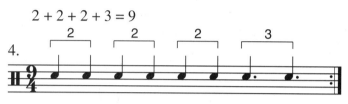

$2 + 3 + 2 + 2 = 9$

5.
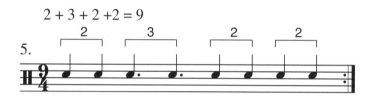

$3 + 3 + 3 = 9$

6.

If the tempo is very fast, you can count or think of the various 2s and 3s as short and long, respectively. Trumpeter, composer, bandleader and musical visionary Don Ellis pioneered the use of odd time signatures and took it further than anyone else I can think of—to the extent, even, of writing one song that had 172 beats per bar! The term "odd" does not mean that the meters are "strange or weird, but rather that they are derived from odd numbers: 5, 7, 9, 11, 13, etc."[20]

The way Don Ellis figured it, if a song of folk-music origin from Turkey or Greece that was in "9" felt natural in a subdivision scheme of 2-2-2-3, it would "then be possible to play in meters of even longer length, and this led to the development of such meters as 3-3-2-2-2-1-2-2-2 (19)."[21]

Don Ellis, 1934–1978

Here is the metric basis for a song that was brought into Don's band by Bulgarian pianist and composer Milcho Leviev. Based on a folk tune, this rhythm cycle contains 33 beats to the bar—and the way those guys played it, it swung!

---

[20] Don Ellis, *The New Rhythm Book* (Ellis Music Enterprises, 1972), p. 11. Sadly, this book is now out of print.

[21] Ibid, p. 6.

As Don Ellis explained (and how the Ellis Band and Stan Kenton Orchestra composer Hank Levy taught me), it is often easier to think of the various 2s and 3s in terms of "short" and "long" as opposed to trying to count each beat. At a fast tempo, that would be impossible ("Because the pattern is so fast, it's almost like memorizing a melody, except in this case you're memorizing the feel of a rhythm.) Usually the longs [3s] are stressed."[22]

While 33/16 sounds sexy, 33/8 is an easier meter to notate and read. Here is a drumming pattern suggested by long-time Ellis drummer (and noted educator) Ralph Humphrey for the tune "Bulgarian Bulge," also known as "Bulgarian Boogie."

R L R L R L R L R L L R L R L R L R L R L R L R L L R L R L L R L R

Fun! Practice this, concentrate, and you'll be swinging in 33 in no time![23]

Inspired by such rhythmic possibilities as well as the haunting sound and ethos of Bulgarian choral music, I decided to try my hand at writing a piece of music in this style. Improvising the rhythmic and chordal scheme at the piano, I intuitively came up with something that sounded "ethnic" in odd time, but proved in reality to work itself out in good old 6/4. I titled the tune "Bulgaria," and I have recorded this with my piano trio and also with the WDR Big Band in Cologne, Germany.

For the most part, the tune sounds as if it is written in some form of "5." Notice the various groupings of 2s and 3s that suggest this:

Combining the odds and evens within a framework of 6/4 seemed to give the song its best chance for swinging.

---

22 Ibid, p. 46.

23 The two best-known drummers to have worked with Don Ellis were the late Steve Bohannon (probably one of the greatest drummers I have ever heard) and the great Ralph Humphrey. They could breathe fire and a complete sense of naturalness into this music. I recommend you find some Don Ellis big band recordings and check them out.

The tune on the following page is included on the *Drumset Essentials 3* CD, as both a live trio performance (from the album *Live at Rocco* with Alan Pasqua and Dave Carpenter) as well as a play-along track (with the same two musicians).

For most small-group (e.g., piano trio) rehearsals or gigs, you'll be presented with a lead sheet as opposed to a proper drum part. You can pretty much make up your part as you go along! This lead sheet should give you all the information you need in order to play along with the band. Your options include either catching all of the various subdivisions, or playing over the larger form of the rhythm (i.e., in a more sweeping 6/4). The idea when playing *any* type of meter or beat is to "see" and "hear" the big picture. Listening is the easiest way to achieve this.

The improvisation in both recordings is in 4/4 (more or less). The count-off by pianist Alan Pasqua is in a "fast" 4/4 (double time). The open drum solo on the *Rocco* recording is actually one of my favorites. I was inspired that night by my good friend Vinnie Colaiuta's presence at the gig! I hope you can hear and enjoy some of the thematic development, tension-and-release devices, and general drum "schtuff" (as my father used to say) that I used in this performance.[24]

---

[24] An additional version of this song can be heard on my ECM album *Time Being*, as well as the Fuzzy Music compilation *Behind Closed Doors, Vol. 1*. On that recording, I play a big band arrangement of the tune by Bill Dobbins with the WDR Big Band and guest vibraphonist Mike Mainieri.

BULGARIA

Track 3 (w/drums)
Track 9 (w/o drums)

PETER ERSKINE

FREE IMPROVISATION . . .

*R*ecommended Study and Practice Methods for Odd-Time Music

In *The New Rhythm Book*, author Don Ellis outlines an exercise regimen that is very useful towards becoming more comfortable with odd-time meters. It involves the use of clapping the subdivisions as well as counting the subdivisions (such as 1-2-3 1-2 1-2 for a measure of 7/4). He then instructs the student to both clap and count together:

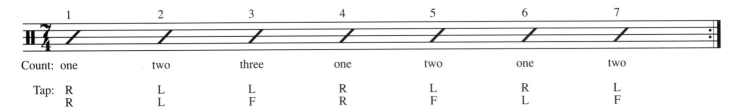

Count: one   two   three   one   two   one   two

Tap: R   L   L   R   L   R   L
      R   L   F   R   F   L   F

The next exercise becomes slightly more difficult, because we are now going to count in double speed against the original claps using the subdivision 3-2-2. Keep the claps as in the single speed (above), and when that becomes comfortable, double the count against the single-speed claps!

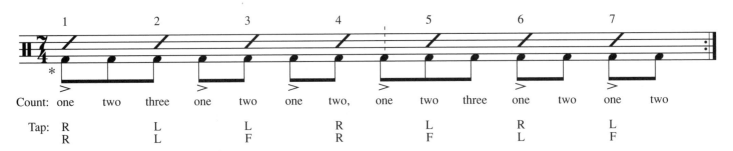

Count: one   two   three   one   two   one   two,   one   two   three   one   two   one   two

Tap: R   L   L   R   L   R   L
      R   L   F   R   F   L   F

*Indications for right foot are the author's additions.

Now you're really learning how to execute and feel two separate rhythms at once. Your hands are clapping a 7/4 and you're reciting two 7/8s against the original 7/4. When you can do this, you've broken the time barrier...[25]

In terms of time signatures, you can use this technique with any metric challenge. Thinking and getting comfortable with two levels of rhythmic awareness works just as well in 4/4 as it does in 13/8.

In the same book, pianist Milcho Leviev offers the following insight into how he and his fellow musicians on both the Ellis band **and** in Bulgaria treat subdivisions and their accents. While the tendency with any subdivision at first is to emphasize the downbeats of each subdivided group, the music will oftentimes swing or rock more if the concept that follows is observed.

---

[25] Don Ellis, *The New Rhythm Book* (Ellis Music Enterprises, 1972), p. 20.

When dealing with groupings of 2s and 3s, the three-note subdivision will be accented more heavily...

...and will be further subdivided by means of an emphasis or heavy accent on its second or third note:

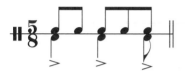   or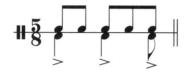

> *In the latter, the third accent sometimes is the heaviest one:*
>
>
>
> *The feeling, however, is still 2+3, not 3+2! That's one of the secrets to playing this music. We have something similar in jazz or rock when we accent the 2nd and 4th beat in a 4/4 measure, and we never get lost, we feel the downbeat...*[26]

Good advice. An additional bit of wisdom from Mr. Ellis:

> *Singing is very important, because if you cannot sing a phrase and feel it correctly, there is no way you'll be able to play it on your instrument. I find if you keep practicing in this manner, progress comes relatively quickly.*[27]

The combined disciplines of both singing and playing can really get your learning juices flowing, and you can devise any number of variations and applications of this practice. Another point I'd like to make is that it is possible and beneficial to practice AWAY from the drumset. Musical understanding comes from more than the mere movement of the hands.

Despite the complexities of much of the Ellis library of music, Don was a gifted melodist as well as a rhythmic guru, and he composed some tremendously heartfelt music.

I close this part of the book with one more quote from Don Ellis:

> *Among the most difficult things to do well in music are to really swing, and to compose or improvise a beautiful, simple melody. I maintain that it is much easier to write or play a lot of fast notes (which may appear to be very difficult but probably have little depth of meaning), than to do something really simple and beautiful, which is at the same time new and fresh.*[28]

Amen.

Recommended Reading

Modern Reading Text in 4/4 by Louie Bellson and Gil Breines

Odd Time Reading Text by Louie Bellson and Gil Breines

Even in the Odds by Ralph Humphrey

---

[26] Ibid., pp. 89–90.

[27] Ibid, p. 14.

[28] Ibid, p. 87.

This big-band chart in 7/4 was composed and arranged by Bill Dobbins, and recorded in Germany with the WDR Big Band. Since we did this all in one room, I couldn't include a mix on this CD without drums, but I thought you might find it enjoyable and instructive to listen and follow along. The 7/4 meter is subdivided 2-2-3.

Loose Your Life
(And It Will Surely Find You)

Track 4 (w/drums)

BILL DOBBINS

This trio tune was originally composed as a study in tone rows, and it does sound fairly modern, particularly in the freely rendered rhythms in the piano. Meanwhile, the bass walks in half time, and the drummer is free to compose rhythms and melodies as he or she likes during the opening section and solo.

Consider these thoughts: "Space is the place," as a jazzer once put it.

"We always solo, and we never solo," as Joe Zawinul once put it about the group Weather Report. Combined with his advice to me to "always compose when you play," you've got a good set of guidelines with which to approach this or any other piece.

The following drum chart has the piano melody rhythm indicated above the staff beginning at measure 33. Remember to listen to what the rest of the band is doing.

DRUMS

MEANWHILE

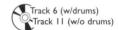
Track 6 (w/drums)
Track 11 (w/o drums)

PETER ERSKINE

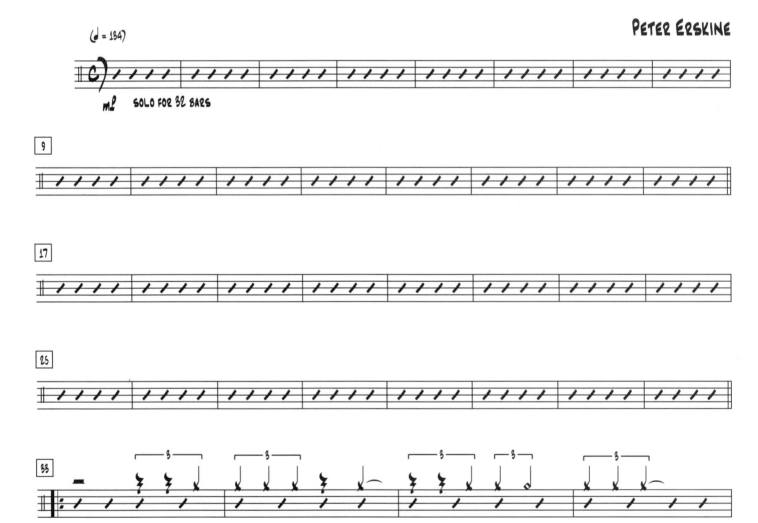

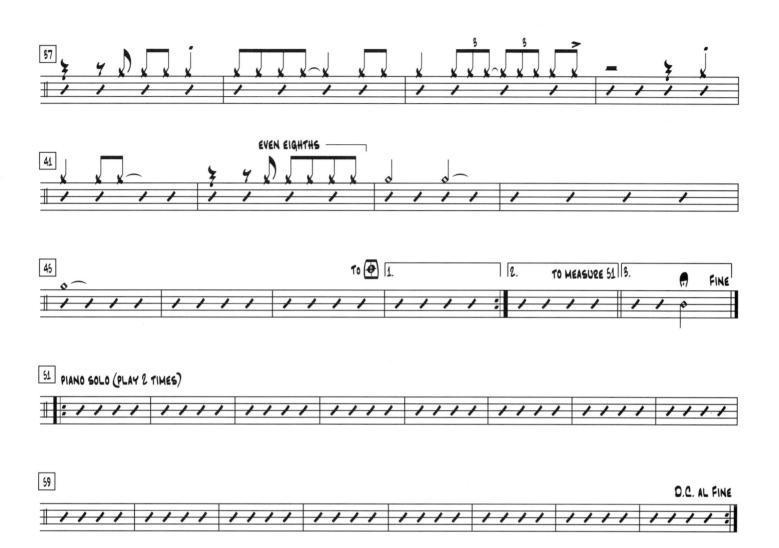

This is a New Orleans/second-line kind of groove I recorded with the Lounge Art Ensemble, playing a stand-up "cocktail kit." I wrote the song, dedicated to all you "cats and kittens" out there. Funky, with the emphasis on f-u-n.

We've included part of the drum intro on the play-along track to get things started, and then you're on your own. A tambourine accompaniment will be your guide, and a lead sheet is provided so you can read the song's form.

Cats & Kittens

(Peter Erskine's Intro/Beat)

Track 5 (w/drums)
Track 10 (w/o drums)

Transcribed by
Matt Slocum

Cats & Kittens

Track 5 (w/drums)
Track 10 (w/o drums)

Peter Erskine

Peter Erskine's Solo
(2:27)

Cats & Kittens

 Track 5 (w/drums)
Track 10 (w/o drums)

Transcribed by
Matt Slocum

*1 Listen to recording for change of speed of double strokes and varied stickings.

SOME TIPS...
How to Get Better

"Getting better" is not just an additive or building process by which one accumulates skills. It is also a shedding process, whereby the developing musician and artist must (and will want to) leave some things behind. One way or the other, "getting better" is about "letting go."

Any craft, however, that involves mechanical motion or requires some measure of dexterity can be improved upon by practice. Repetitive exercises build muscle, and muscle provides "chops." There are two stereotypical images of athletic and muscular achievement: One is of the large, muscle-bound body trainer, and the other is of the accomplished athlete whose prowess comes as much from nimble agility as from muscle mass. Keep those images in mind when you work on your chops. For me, practicing is more about increasing your physical confidence so you can actually relax more when you play, as opposed to merely flexing your muscles.

It's important to establish some sort of routine to your practice sessions. This can be as basic as a set of warm-up exercises that involve single- and double-stroke patterns such as single-stroke rolls, double-stroke rolls and paradiddles:

L R L R L R L R L R L R L R L R

L L R R L L R R L L R R L L R R*

L R L L R L R R L R L L R L R R ...etc.

Note: When the double-stroke roll goes into "buzz" roll territory, the actual speed of the arm and wrist motions slow down. Try to bring the sound that's in your head out of the drum (i.e., **smooth**). Remember—like a wind instrument, the snare drum roll is the drummer's "long tone," and the speed of the arms, hands and wrists is not necessarily dependent upon the tempo of the tune.

Then there's the challenge of playing in unison, **without** flams, on both the practice pad and the various parts of the drumset.

A terrific idea for practicing non-interpretive reading (like snare drum music as opposed to drumset/big band charts, etc.) is this: Take a SIMPLE page of exercises, something that has combinations of quarter and eighth notes, and then play that page at a breakneck tempo by reading. This is terrific for the ol' hand-eye coordination. Practice with your eyes OPEN. Many drummers play the drumset with their eyes closed—bet you don't practice the marimba or timpani with your eyes closed!

Every experience informs the next. Don't get discouraged. Stay inspired. Play what you hear. While practice time is essential for building up your chops, its most important function, I believe, is to build up your self-awareness as a musician and a human being. Remember, too, that you are building and honing a craft. To be good at anything always takes time and effort.

Erskine's Rules

The following are a set of handy tips I hope will be helpful to you.

Erskine's 10 Rules of Drumming

1. Music should be fun.
2. Listen when you play.
3. Breathe deeply.
4. Strive for tone.
5. Develop a good touch.
6. Tune your instrument well.
7. Explore texture and sound.
8. Find your own technique.
9. Think of time, all of the time.
10. Be professional.

Erskine's 12 Points on "How to Make It"

1. Don't forget why you're doing this in the first place.
2. Play with grace, and live in gratitude.
3. Show respect to musicians and your audience.
4. Live in the musical moment.
5. Be prompt.
6. Have the right equipment for the job.
6. Pay attention!
7. Don't make excuses.
8. Get as much experience as possible.
9. Find and embrace your lasting musical values.
10. Don't be afraid to say "no."
11. Keep your ears open.
12. Be polite to your audience.

Peter's Practice Advice

1. Know when to knock off for a break.
2. Slow and steady does it...
3. Focus on a goal and work towards it.
4. Practice simple and basic beats.
5. LONG TONES (whole notes on the ride cymbal or tom; LISTEN to the sound).
6. Work on specific things, and think of specific tempos. Be aware.
7. Compose when you play, and always be musical.
8. Record your practice session, and keep a practice diary or log.
9. Quality is more important than quantity.
10. Warming up is good to do!
11. Speed reading of simple rhythms is good exercise for both your hands and brain.
12. Practice with your eyes OPEN.

Musicality

1. Make the music sound like you're **discovering it for the first time**.
2. Don't play out of habit; **make each note count**.
3. Fills must have a **proper proportion or weight**, acknowledging the musical transition while keeping things moving ahead; **simple and strong works best**.
4. Consider the "hand-off" nature of L/R (and foot) playing for tutti-figure setups (and learn how best to **play between the band arrangement's figures**).
5. **Own the time**. Honor the spaces between notes.
6. Better not to chase one's own tail when playing a solo; **stay relaxed**.
7. **Breathe deeply**; oxygen provides fuel for the muscles and clarity to the brain.
8. **Strive for tone**; consider your sticks' grip (relaxation), rebound, angle and height in relation to the instrument.
9. **Develop a good touch**; let your instrument sing! Think of the concept of folding or tucking your drumbeats into the music.
10. **Stay relaxed and in playing position**, and **keep your hands and sticks down where they're doing their business**!
11. **Find your own voice**.
12. **Go for the emotional aspect of a beat**; don't worry too much about transcriptions.

Quick Tips for Touring:

1. Stay out of trouble when you travel!
2. Drink plenty of water in the air and on the ground.
3. Keep track of your air mileage (those miles come in handy for upgrades and early boarding privileges).
4. Keep track of your business-related expenses.
5. Make certain your spouse or family has your travel itinerary information.
6. Get all business-related agreements or understandings in writing before leaving town.
7. Be prepared, musically.
8. Pack smart: Include appropriate clothing for the weather, for the stage, and for traveling as well as for relaxing. Don't forget a portable umbrella...
9. ID your luggage and instrument(s).
10. Bring an alarm clock and a toothbrush.

TRAVEL SMART

Joe Zawinul gave me this advice when I joined Weather Report: "Always be good to the people who handle your bags and your food." Tip well and be courteous. A smile and generous manners will always make your day more pleasant, and you'll bring happiness to someone else, too! By doing this, you'll receive the best service at airports, hotels and restaurants. Good idea to be polite with local stage techs, as well as with your audience.

Touring is a great way to see the world, meet people and spread the good word about music. It's also a good way to make a living. Play your best every opportunity, and get paid at the end of the job. Safe travels—and don't lose your wallet, tickets or passport!

Weather Report, circa 1980.
From left to right: Wayne Shorter, Joe Zawinul, Peter Erskine, Jaco Pastorius, Bobby Thomas, Jr.

*A*fterword

When I was six years old, I finally had the opportunity to meet drumming legend Gene Krupa. He was appearing at the Steel Pier ballroom in Atlantic City, and my oldest sister, Lois (who was 15 at the time), took me to see him play. When she saw where his dressing room was located, she took me in tow and knocked on his door. He was alone in the room and answered, kindly inviting us in. She did a short song and dance routine about how I was this terrific young drummer and Gene finally said, as he handed me a pair of drumsticks and pointed to a chair, "Show me what you can do, Kid." I had never played on a wooden chair before, but I gulped, grabbed the sticks and fumbled something on the seat of the chair's surface with Mr. Krupa's drumsticks. When I looked up at him, Gene Krupa smiled, nodded his head and said "Yeah, Kid … yeah!"

Gene played a knockout set at that afternoon matinee, and gave this kid drummer a memorable moment he would never forget. May you enjoy all of your musical moments.

Peter showing what he can do on a Yamaha HipGig drumset for a percussion class at his high school alma mater, the Interlochen Arts Academy, in Michigan, 2003.

About the Recordings

Piano trio play-alongs and Aaron Serfaty demonstration examples recorded at Puck Productions, Santa Monica, CA, by Brian Risner

Lounge Art Ensemble play-alongs remixed by Rich Breen

Horn of Puente

Gordon Goodwin's Big Phat Band

From *Property of Gordon Goodwin's Big Phat Band XXL* (B0000CABHC), courtesy of Belwin-Mills Publishing Corp. & Warner Brothers Publications U.S. Inc.
    Saxes: Eric Marienthal, Sal Lozano, Brian Scanlon, Jeff Driskill, Jay Mason
    Trumpets: Wayne Bergeron (solo), Dan Fornero, Stan Martin, Dan Savant
    Trombones: Andy Martin, Alex Iles, Steve Holtman, Craig Ware
    Bass: Richard Shaw
    Guitar: Grant Geissman
    Percussion: Luis Conte
    Piano: Gordon Goodwin
    Drums: Peter Erskine
    Produced by Gordon Goodwin and Dan Savant

Manny's Setup

    Piano: Otmaro Ruiz
    Bass: Eddie Resto
    Clave: Aaron Serfaty

Loose Your Life (and It Will Surely Find You)

Featuring the WDR Big Band

From *Prism* (2000011), courtesy of Advance Music, Bill Dobbins
    Saxes: Heiner Wiberny, Harald Rosenstein, Olivier Peters, Rölf Römer, Jens Neufang
    Trumpets: Andy Haderer, Rob Bruynen, Klaus Osterloh, Rick Kiefer, John Marshall
    Trombones: Dave Horler, Ludwig Nuss, Bernt Laukamp, Lucas Schmid
    Bass: John Goldsby
    Guitar: Paul Shigihara
    Piano: Frank Chastenier
    Drums and percussion: Peter Erskine
    Recorded at Studio 4, WDR Radiofunkhaus, Cologne, Germany
    Please visit www.advancemusic.com concerning ordering information for the CD and big band chart.

Cats & Kittens

The Lounge Art Ensemble

From *Lava Jazz* (PEPCD004), courtesy of Fuzzy Music
    Saxophones: Bob Sheppard
    Bass: Dave Carpenter
    Drums and percussion: Peter Erskine
    Recorded by Bernie Kirsh at Mad Hatter Studios

Summer's Waltz and Meanwhile

From *Badlands* (PEPCD011), courtesy of Fuzzy Music
    Piano: Alan Pasqua
    Bass: Dave Carpenter
    Drums: Peter Erskine
    Recorded at Puck Productions, Santa Monica, CA
    Engineered by Brian Risner
    Mixed by Rich Breen

Bulgaria

From *Live at Rocco* (PEPCD007), courtesy of Fuzzy Music
    Piano: Alan Pasqua
    Bass: Dave Carpenter
    Drums: Peter Erskine
    Recorded and mixed by Rich Breen